The Paranormal Part of Me

Copyright © 2024 Cynthia McNamara. All Rights Reserved

No parts of this book may be used, sold, or reproduced without the written consent of the copyright owner.

INTRODUCTION	5
WHAT IS PARANORMAL ANYWAY?	14
WHY ARE WE HERE?	25
IN THE BEGINNING	35
(DON'T SAY YOUR PARENTS NEVER GAVE YOU ANYTHING)	35
BEFORE IT BEGAN	43
CRASH, BANG, BOO…	49
GRANDMA, I LOVE YOU BUT PLEASE, DON'T COME SEE ME…	55
PERCHANCE TO DREAM	59
HEAVY FOOTSTEPS	60
GOING UP?	64
ARE THERE MESSAGES IN DREAMS?	72
A SNOWY PREMONITION	73
VOICES ON THE WIND	77
EVOLUTION OF THE SHADOW MAN	82
SOMETIMES YOU CONDUIT, AND SOMETIMES YOU CON'T…	92
EVIL WHISPERS	96
TERRORS IN THE NIGHT (AND SOMETIMES THE DAY)	99
WHAT DID HE GET HIMSELF INTO?	101
DÉJÀ VU ALL OVER AGAIN	109

MY DAUGHTER'S GROUND HOG DAYS	113
IF YOU HAVE GHOSTS…	116
WHO ARE YOU GONNA CALL?	126
PAX ET QUIETAM	130
SPEAKING OF FAMILY: MOM	131
WHAT IS ITC?	153
"THE DAY SCIENCE BEGINS TO STUDY NON-PHYSICAL PHENOMENA, IT WILL MAKE MORE PROGRESS IN ONE DECADE THAN IN ALL THE PREVIOUS CENTURIES OF ITS EXISTENCE."	153
TESLA TALKED TO ALIENS	158
WHAT IS A GHOST BOX?	162
TAKING MY SHOW ON THE…TUBE	166
LONG LOST LOVE	174
A QUESTION FROM BEYOND	179
STANDING GUARD FOR ETERNITY	184
ABANDONED FARMHOUSE	189
A HAND ON MY SHOULDER	194
WHY I DO THIS	202
HOW I PERFORM A GHOST BOX SESSION	210
DEMONS AND THE PARANORMAL ENTERTAINER	217
IT'S NOT WHAT YOU BELIEVE, IT'S WHAT YOU BELIEVE MIGHT BE POSSIBLE	222

OCCAM'S RAZOR	**228**
MY PARANORMAL PARTNER IN CRIME: DR. RAY	**232**
HAUNTED SACH'S BRIDGE, GETTYSBURG	**246**
LATE NIGHT XTREME GHOST HUNT	**253**
BONAVENTURE CEMETERY	**258**
IN CONCLUSION	**264**
ONE MORE THOUGHT	**270**

For my family. Thanks for putting up with me.

Introduction

I used to sleep like the dead.

When I was a teenager, I convinced my mother to let my grandfather paint my bedroom deep, midnight blue. On a moonless night, it was like lying in a sensory deprivation tank. I felt comfortable and safe in my blacked-out cocoon.

I wasn't trying to make any sort of statement. True, I had transitioned out of my French provincial four-poster bed to a simple, brass headboard but this was the 1970s, long before "emo" became a thing. I respected my parents, loved my brothers (even if they drove me nuts) and I had no reason to rebel.

My original request was to have the room painted black, but my mother put the absolute kibosh on that idea. Finally, I was able to convince her and midnight blue it was painted. To me, every night felt like I was camping under a starless sky and the darkness felt like a weighted blanket, impenetrable and safe. It had nothing to do with teenage angst. I just loved to sleep in dark room.

In 1975, when I was 15 years old and about 10 years into my experiences, I would be lying in bed, wrapped in my blanket of darkness, asleep, when something would wake me. I would look around the room. The house was silent, my parents and my brothers asleep, and no noise was coming from outside.

Out of the darkness I would hear a lilting voice call to me.

Whenever this happened, I would get a strange sensation in my ears, as if I was suddenly standing in a bubble. I'll tell you more about the significance of that later when I talk about my actual experiences with spirit contact.

This name calling went on throughout the 70's and 80's.

This was a time when you didn't discuss these things openly for fear of being thought unhinged. I honestly never told another soul about hearing my name called until after I graduated college in 1983. I was having a discussion with one of my sorority sisters. As it turned out, she had very similar experiences throughout her youth. But that was as far as that conversation went.

It would be many years before all things paranormal would become part of the lexicon. The very popular television show, Ghost Adventures, premiered in 2008 and I believe that was the beginning of it becoming normalized, albeit as a form of entertainment. It is still considered pseudoscience, which is defined in the Oxford dictionary as beliefs or practices "mistakenly" regarded as being based on scientific method.

The change in societal opinions about the paranormal created a huge change in my life. Where it had always been something I did not bring up when in mixed company, it was now a great party starter. Granted, most of the time at gatherings it would be my husband who would pull me over to a group of people, saying "guess what my wife does?"

Amazingly, what happens most of the time now is that folks are very eager to talk about the paranormal and share their experiences. Even the skeptics in a group who generally open with "I don't believe in ghosts" will want to share "this one thing" that happened to them that they cannot explain. Then they look at me for an explanation, even though they don't necessarily want to believe what I might have to say.

Here is what I always tell skeptics. I respect their skepticism because we, as people who have experienced and investigated what we consider to be paranormal, ask the very same questions, every single day, every time we do a session. We have no answers yet. I tell them to keep being skeptical because it is not a matter of what you believe. It is a matter of what you believe might be possible.

This book is meant to show you, and anyone else who has walked a similar path, that the paranormal experiences I have had do not define me. I have had a normal life. In fact, it has probably been a painfully normal life. I have a family, a successful business, and a couple of children. I have even raised a couple of dogs.

And I have had paranormal experiences. The paranormal is just a part of who I am.

My life has been just like yours. There have been ups and downs, happiness and sadness, the good, the bad and the ugly. But for the most part, it has been good. I love my family. I love my friends. I care about the environment. I worry about the world. I try to keep my house clean, which never seems to work. I go to work every day. I come home most nights and make dinner. Sometimes we go to the movies. Sometimes we go on vacation. I now have two beautiful grandchildren whom I adore. It's all good.

I also believe a sense of humor is crucial, not only in dealing with these experiences, but in every facet of our lives. It is vital to help us weather the peaks and valleys, the ebb and flow, the good, the not-so-good, and the Covid. Any story I tell will always be peppered with a bit of humor and so shall this book, because if we can't laugh, we'll cry. I prefer the former.

My goal is to tell my story. I hope that you will find it interesting, enjoyable, enlightening, and funny. I would like to share my life and show you how the paranormal has been a part of it since I was five years old. I am 63 years old now and, while it has been a constant in my life, it is just a small part of who I am.

The important thing to take away from this book besides, hopefully, that I'm a halfway decent writer and that you got a chuckle out of it, is that the paranormal doesn't define me or any of us. It is not on my mind every hour of every day. It is just one part, the paranormal part of me.

What is Paranormal anyway?

par·a·nor·mal
/ˌperəˈnôrm(ə)l/

adjective
1. denoting events or phenomena such as telekinesis or clairvoyance that are beyond the scope of normal scientific understanding.

It is easy to take for granted those things that are defined as "normal". They are the usual, the regular, the day-to-day occurrences and chapters of a life that make sense based on everything we have either been taught or have experienced before. The average human being does not consider whether there is a scientific basis for the daily, weekly, monthly or even yearly, events they witness or are a part of throughout their lifetime. I find it amusing that the Oxford definition of "paranormal" includes telekinesis and clairvoyance. It seems a bit extreme to reference moving things with your mind or reading other's thoughts in order to emphasize the "normalcy" of a scientific approach.

What passes as normal, then, for most people, are things they have become used to, accustomed to; those things that are a constant in their life from a very early age on. The things, and experiences that no longer surprise them.

Of course, there is the Oxford definition for "normal" as well. It is defined as anything that "conforms to a standard; is usual, typical, or expected", just as I have noted.

Where we often get tripped up is in thinking that "paranormal" is the opposite of "normal". It is not.

The prefix "para" is borrowed from the Greek language, and generally results in a derivative word meaning "at or to one side of, beside, or side by side" the original. Based on this etymology, "paranormal" is not opposite of "normal", but a sister (or brother) that walks beside (or perhaps a few paces behind).

But what if a person's paranormal experiences begin at a very young age? What if they begin before the age of episodic memory, those first memories so fleeting, tucked away in our minds during childhood? What if they, then, continue throughout that person's life and thus are no longer a surprise when they do occur?

Do they then become that person's base line? Their "normal"?

Our modern-day definition of paranormal results, in large part, from the various forms of entertainment available, with story lines based on some writer's idea of its meaning. I am, of course, referring to the many television shows dedicated to an overly emotional quest for contact with "the other side": spirits of those who have passed on. There are movies as well, but the majority market share is populated by a plethora of excitable personalities who seem to be surprised when they encounter exactly what they were seeking.

I understand the nature of entertainment and the constant battle to maintain an audience's attention to ensure a program's success, i.e., continue to be worthy of the dollars spent by the advertisers that, in turn, pay the salaries of the personalities/actors/film crew/etc. But their level of surprise and shock always seem disingenuous to me. Yes, the shows are very entertaining, and I have watched a few of them. But I make this statement based on my own personal experiences, which I will describe for you in depth, with many interesting examples, in the following chapters. All of this began when I was five years old.

My earliest encounters will be told in

retrospect. Since I was so young and had no concept of the paranormal, I became convinced I was a child prone to bad dreams. When I was older, and as a result of a barrage of unsolicited spiritual contact in my twenties, any confusion or consternation I felt as a result of my "bad dreams" was replaced by aggravation. I had no control over what was happening to me. However, once I learned to draw a line in the ethereal sand and close the door that I didn't even know had been opened, everything changed.

That is a story for another chapter. And why shouldn't you be interested in the paranormal? We humans are intrigued by the things we can't explain or have explained to us in a manner that immediately makes perfect sense.

We are seekers. I know I am a seeker. I feel as if I'm always looking for something. On a day-to-day basis, my family will come to me when they can't find something. It seems I'm the only one who really knows how to look for the lost things. I have a process and they mock me for it. But I find things. The problem is, I drive myself nuts until I've found it.

If I misplace an item, which I seem to do more of these days, I'll look for it before I can move onto another task.

I will have days where I find everything. I will even ask everyone in the household, "are you missing anything, because today is one of those days!"

I also suffer from a strange phenomenon. If I put something down or away with my left hand, I won't remember where I put it. Using my right hand, I have no problem. As a result, I try to use both hands when putting anything down. My doctor made some interesting "hmm" sounds when I told her about it, but I don't think it means much. It's just frustrating.

I also don't know how I got so off track.

The point I am trying to make is this: the term paranormal is subjective. In my opinion, it means different things to different people. Your normal and my normal are probably similar in many ways and yet vastly different in others. By all outward appearances, I am a well-adjusted, suburban, adult woman. I don't have a criminal record, I have all my teeth, and my house is neat but in a perpetual state of needing to be cleaned.

I also attempt to talk to the dead.

For me, this is part of my normal, and has been for over 50 years.

I wanted to make one more point about the paranormal. With the popularization of "ghost hunt" shows, some folks may think that those who experience these phenomena live in a vacuum, have a one-track mind, or are wholly obsessed with everything paranormal. This is far from the truth, and one of the main reasons for my writing these stories down here.

My paranormal experiences are just one part of me. They are one part of a very full, and fulfilling, non-paranormal life. They always have been. But, for most of my life, I did not publicly share them. This may have been for fear of being thought I had gone over the side of my dinghy but, for the most part, it was because they did not consume my day-to-day life. They still do not.

I've wracked my brain for some way to explain this to you. The best way, well maybe not the best but it will suffice, is to liken them to acid reflux. It comes and goes unbidden, and you seek out remedies, never knowing when it may strike. Most people don't have it, and many who do don't discuss it because it's embarrassing. But it is part of you, for better or for worse. So, you deal with the flareups, and you move on. You probably don't make YouTube videos about it, but I never said it was a perfect analogy.

This book will chronicle my experiences throughout my "normal", considerably uneventful life and my attempts in recent years to communicate beyond the veil. Perhaps reading my stories will demonstrate that the veil is thinner than we realize and that even common folk like me can pierce it.

I hope you enjoy my stories.

Why Are We Here?

When I decided to write this book, to finally put down in print my lifetime of paranormal experiences, the first question I asked myself (and am still asking myself) is: where do I begin?

If you've ever written anything, a research paper, a job resignation letter, maybe even an anniversary card to a loved one, you've pondered this same question.

I couldn't decide. Do I begin with the current state of paranormal research, or do I escort you through the early years when my experiences were chalked up to nightmares and nothing more? I've chosen the latter and can only hope you enjoy the journey. There are some good stories here.

But this thought process begs another question: how do these things start in the first place? How does one begin to experience strange events that are scientifically, or even logically unexplainable? For this book, I will draw from my own personal experiences and possibly of those people closest to me who have agreed to share their stories as well.

There are so many anecdotal stories that have made the rounds down through history which are now considered to be fact by many. Over time, even urban legends begin to take on the ring of, at the very least, possibility. Each legend is basically a theory which, by definition, is both true and not true until it is either proven or disproven.

I am going to dull down quantum mechanics (just for one moment) to make a point about theories. In 1935, Erwin Schrödinger fashioned a rebuttal to Albert Einstein who opined that one system or atom, or anything, could not exist in more than one state at one time. The rebuttal came in the form of a thought experiment in which a cat (a hypothetical cat!) would be placed in a box with a flask of poison and a radioactive source. The box would then be sealed. If an internal monitor were to detect radioactivity, the flask would break and, well, it would not be good for

Schrödinger's cat.

The basis of the model was this: without opening the box, we can theorize that the cat is both still alive and no longer with us. It exists in two states. It is called the paradox of superposition and that is your dose of quantum physics for today.

My point is, any theory that has yet to be confirmed or scientifically disproved, is fact or fiction based on any given person's mindset. To offhandedly discount them, while often a defense against the unknown, is anyone's right. Conversely, so is doing the opposite.

Just because you can't prove Bigfoots exist doesn't mean we must automatically believe they do not. The same goes for UFOs, though I must confess, I am one of those people who do not want there to be alien life visiting us in all their probing glory. If they can construct a way to get here, they are much smarter than we and that does not bode well for our species. Honestly, we have enough going on here to keep us busy for another millennium. Besides any threat of a much more intelligent, interplanetary race of gooey green/grey beings hell bent on proving their greater military ability, we don't need to be worrying about which fast food joint will jump the wormhole first.

Before I go any further, I want to acknowledge that there are probably those of you who are members of the neuroscientific community who will hold a very different opinion of the stories I'm about to tell. Much respect is due the scientists of the world and I do not doubt that, in some instances, paranormal experiences can be the result of "the dynamic matrix of chemical and electromagnetic events within the human brain." [1] The footnoted article is very interesting. Bring your dictionary. I'm still trying to figure out if it means I'm a bit "teched" in the head. But, lacking any other symptoms that might lean toward that diagnosis, and considering myself a stable human being, I'll forego that determination at this time and

---

[1] The Neuropsychiatry of Paranormal Experiences
Michael A. Persinger, Ph.D., C.Psych.
Published Online:1 Nov 2001
https://neuro.psychiatryonline.org/doi/full/10.1176/jnp.13.4.515

simply regale you with my own life stories.

Over the years, I've had folks share with me, both in person and online, how and when they began to have paranormal experiences. Their accounts vary, with most admitting they had them all their lives. I've also met countless skeptics who proudly admit they do not believe in the paranormal and then will go on to tell me about that one experience they had that they can't explain. It is generally just something that happened out of the blue that they continue to try to rationalize but simply cannot explain away.

One of those people is my husband.

My husband has never believed in ghosts or spirits or the paranormal. When he was growing up, the stairs that used to creak at night under invisible feet in the old Victorian painted lady he and his family lived in were explained away by his civil engineer father as a 200-year-old house still settling. He managed to get to his 54th year before having an experience. Now, six years later, he is still trying to make sense of it.

One dark night, he was driving home from the firehouse (he's a volunteer firefighter). It was a four-mile trip, and he was on one of our many winding town roads. There are no streetlamps and at one point you come to a spot where there are two cemeteries, one on each side of the road, across from each other. I've even visited them for my YouTube channel. They are very old and no longer accepting new residents.

On the night in question, there was no moon and no other vehicles passed him however, as he drove between the two graveyards, he swears he witnessed two apparitions of women in 19th century dresses float across the road, side by side. He said it was as if they were taking a walk together and they made no notice of him. But he did remember that they had no feet. The women appeared from the knees up.

That was his first experience. There's no explanation for why he would suddenly have one after a lifetime of nothing. We had been married for twenty-nine years at that point, and he knew of me and my family's history all that time, so why now?

The answer is, there is no answer. Some people have vague memories of something from their childhood that spooked them: a scary camp ghost story, Bloody Mary in the mirror at sleepover parties, Ouija board seances. But the most common catalyst I know of, and I mean personally, is a traumatic event. That is where my story begins.

In the Beginning
(Don't say your parents never gave you anything)

My mother's mother, my nana, was named Margaret, but my grandfather always called her Margie. Her parents came to America from the north of Italy and her father went back there when her mother died to bring back his cousin, whom he then married. Margie and her siblings hated their stepmother so much that when my nana and grandpa married, they took all of them in and raised them.

My nana was the matriarch of our family. She worked in the garment district in

New York City doing piecework making lady's underwear while my grandfather plastered walls. She raised her brothers and sisters, her own children and me and my brothers. We spent so much time at the apartment on Lafontaine Avenue in the Bronx that it was like our second home. She was a force to be reckoned with.

And she could see the future.

The definition of a premonition is: "a strong feeling that something is about to happen, especially something unpleasant." Fittingly, one of the similar words offered by Oxford is "foreboding". The reason for this is simple, and if you've ever had a premonition, you will be able to attest to the same. They rarely offer a glimpse of pleasant occurrences.

The reason I tell you about my nana is because of her gift, if you want to call it that. It is something she handed down to my mother. My mother, it seems, did the same for me. Or to me. It depends on how you look at it. For most of my early life, I did not consider it a gift. Let me go back a bit further.

My mother never learned to speak Italian. My grandparents wanted her to be an American. It's a pity, really. I feel we missed out on being bilingual, which is a great asset in the world today. She also had a difficult time as a child. It seemed she was anemic and had a heart condition that was never traced back to the black coffee she drank every day from the time she was five years old. We've come a long way baby!

When my mother speaks of her childhood, it is punctuated by the years of doctor visits and all she endured to overcome her confusing ailment.

It is often opined that certain parapsychological abilities can begin or be brought on by a traumatic event or struggle. Perhaps that is why, when her body finally matured past the issues that plagued her as a child, she began to have similar experiences as her mother. She also discovered that she could read tea leaves. Accurately.

I know this sounds like a very old-fashioned parlor game to most people. With the prevalence these days of prebagged tea, the use of loose tea that ends up at the bottom of a cup is rare. I know this is a generalization as it seems to be making a resurgence. I, myself, have owned a few tea diffusers. They looked really cool on my kitchen shelves, and I never once used any of them.

The idea of letting tea leaves settle to the bottom of a teacup and then divining meaning from their placement is no longer in vogue. Still, in the 1940s and 50s it was still quite popular.

My mother was born in 1935. One evening when she was in her 20s, she was with some of her friends having a meal. I don't know what meal it was, however one of the ladies was awaiting the arrival of her boyfriend, or husband who was running a bit late. According to my mother, there was nothing out of the ordinary. It was just some friends coming together over food and coffee. And tea.

When the meal was over and the cups were empty, my mother picked up her friend's teacup and looked at the leaves in the bottom. She remembers turning the cup a time or two and an image in the drying leaves started to stand out.

Now, remember what I said about premonitions and how they are rarely about happy things?

Mom told me that what she saw didn't make much sense, but that she shared it with her friends none the less. What she saw in the leaves appeared to be a car, but the car seemed to have something spewing from the back of it. In my mind, I liken it to those pictures of unicorns drawn with rainbows coming out of their bottoms.

When she told her friends, they laughed because it made no sense. But mom says she felt a terrible foreboding. She knew better.

Not long after, the phone rang.

The young man that was on his way had been in a car accident. Thankfully, he was alright, but his car had been hit hard from behind. It was wrecked.

It turns out that the trunk had been full of toys on their way to be donated. When the two vehicles collided, according to witnesses at the scene, the crushed trunk sprang open and colorful playthings spewed out onto the road.

My mother told me she didn't read tea leaves after that happened.

I was not told of this family trait until I was in my teens. Up until that time, the experiences I had were described to me as bad dreams. I don't blame my mother. Odds are, she was hoping they were just that. Perhaps some of them were. What would one tell a five-year-old child? I'll tell you about how it started for me, and you can decide for yourself.

Before It Began

I don't remember our first apartment. It was on Morris Avenue in the Bronx, but I was just an infant. It's hiding in the recesses of my mind somewhere, but I can only access one distinct, visceral memory.

I remember being very small, about three years old, and my mother had sat me on the floor in front of our black and white television. It was one of those long, wooden consoles that housed the television as well as a record player up top. I remember this piece of furniture because it made the move with us when I was five years old to another place in the

Bronx. It's also the same TV, I am told, I tried to take a hammer to when my father or mother left one lying around, inadvertently.

I also remember watching an old cartoon called Winky Dink, and drawing a bridge for Winky on the plastic sheet your mother would place over the screen during his cartoon shows. If you're not familiar with either a record player or Winky Dink, google them. You'll get a kick out of it.

The memory I am referring to involves me watching the blurry figures on the screen that day while I listened to my mother and other ladies in the kitchen behind me crying. It was November 1963 and President John F. Kennedy had just been killed. Of course, I didn't know this at the time, or for many years to come. I only came to the realization of the gravity of the moment in later years. But the memory is quite vivid.

Our next apartment was on Baychester Avenue, and my memories from there are extensive. I loved this apartment. My bedroom was in the front, and I would sit in the window and watch the traffic. That may sound sad and boring, but I assure you it was not. We lived on a corner at a four-lane intersection that seemed huge to me at the time. I remember the night someone drove right into the living room of the garden apartment diagonally across from us. Good times.

I remember the blackout of 1965

November, sitting at that same window, watching drivers traversing the intersection with the traffic lights out and gasping at every fender bender or near-miss that occurred.

My other favorite memory involves my brother. His bedroom was in the back of the apartment and overlooked the backyard which had a swing set. We enjoyed the swings often with our friends from the block. The building was only two stories high, and our landlords lived below us with one other apartment at ground level.

At one point, the building sold, and the new landlords moved in downstairs. They decided that the backyard was no longer ours to use, and we were locked out.

One lovely summer day, as the landlords and their family were picnicking in our former/now forbidden space below my brother's window, he and I came up with a brilliant plan. We loaded two water pistols and, crouching below the windowsill as to not be seen, we pressed the plastic toys to the screen and began pulling the triggers. We could hear the people below commenting on why they might be feeling raindrops on an otherwise beautiful, sunny day. It was hilarious.

Even all these years later, I can feel the giddy rush of satisfaction and joy which was certainly amplified by the fact that we didn't consider there could be any price to pay. We were living in the moment, and it was glorious.

It was my first taste of the joys of revenge.

Of course, my mother heard our giggles of delight and put a stop to the fun. I can still see her eyes wide with realization as she admonished us under her breath as not to alert the folks below.

I was in the throes of a completely normal childhood but, at some point before the winter of 1965/66, one traumatic incident changed everything.

Crash, Bang, Boo...

The weather had begun to turn cool with the dying of Autumn. It was that in-between time, when mothers contemplated the days to come, stuffing their kids into thick, woolen jackets with gloves attached at the wrist. Our little faces would turn red, not so much from the wind but from the tight hat string tied tightly under our chins.

It was a brisk, sunny day, one of the last that year when I could go outside in just a light windbreaker. It remains vivid in my memory, even these many years later.

Mom and I had just come down the main

staircase from our apartment. I was skipping ahead of her happily as we headed for the front door of the apartment building.

The style of the outer door was one of those that was still popular into the seventies: glass panes above and below with a metal, swirling design on the bottom.

As I skipped in front of my mother, my sneakers caught on the weather stripping along the floor and my momentum launched me through the bottom half of the door. She says it happened so fast there was nothing she could do. I went through the glass pane in a Super Man pose, and the door flew open. When it went as far as it could go, the metal design reversed the momentum and threw me backwards, out of the door and onto the ground.

Then, the glass from the top half of the door slammed down like a guillotine.

I was very lucky, in retrospect. However, this is where my memory kicks in. Mostly what I remember is screaming, and glass, and blood, and white socks.

Every house on the block had a metal fence that separated us from our neighbor. The man who lived next door was home relaxing and when he heard my screams, he ran out of his house in his pure white socks to come to my aid. He never put on his shoes, and he ran right into all the glass and blood on the ground, picked me up, and got me in a car. I was whisked to Misericordia hospital. There, I was cleaned up, stitched up, and bandaged. I've blocked that part out.

My next memory is coming home with a cast on my arm. It was applied because I was so young, and they wanted to give my arm a chance to heal a bit. I have a distinct memory of returning to my bedroom and looking in the mirror atop my dresser. The light in the room was fading with the day, but something felt different. Of course, I had been through a lot, but I can still recall my room and the air around me feeling different. I had no idea.

My parents and my grandma Ellen, my dad's mother, wanted to cheer me up after the accident. They meant well when they brought home the life-sized doll. She had blonde hair, just like me, and was my height. It was really a sweet thing to do, albeit a little creepy, looking back. But I didn't think so at the time. I thought it was lovely.

Unfortunately, I'm told the doll had to go at one point after I told my parents she was trying to talk to me. I do not remember this myself, but my mother is not one to make up tall tales.

Then came the strange dreams. I have done some reading as an adult and know that most children will experience either a ghost, skeleton, or witch dream sometime during their childhood. Looking back at my "dream" of a small, flying witch that, one night, cackled at me and closed my door, I can understand that a five year old me would believe my mother when she said it was just that, a bad dream.

As I grew older, I remember my mother telling me this often. I don't remember many of the dreams, but a few stand out because they stayed with me for over twenty years.

It wasn't until I was around thirteen years old that I was told of the matriarchal family history. When I was finally enlightened, a lot of things started to make sense. Well, as much sense as something like this can make, anyway.

Grandma, I love you but please, don't come see me…

I used to say my prayers every night before bed, without fail. I would include all of my loved ones in my petitions, including Grandma Ellen. I found out later in my life that she had her own demons to deal with, including my alcoholic grandfather who I was never allowed to meet. But to me she was a kind, quiet woman and I adored her.

Ellen Larson was a soft-spoken woman who had come to the United States via Ellis Island from Norway when she was young. My father had me learn to sing "Wonderful

Copenhagen" for her, and him and anyone else that would listen at family gatherings.

She came to stay with us when I was about eight years old, and she slept in my bedroom while I bunked in my brothers in the back of the apartment. I can still picture her lying on my bed, resting. I don't have my own memory of the ambulance crew that took her to the hospital, which is odd because that was the last time I was in her physical company.

The very last time I saw her, she was standing in a third story window of a large brick building wearing a white dressing gown and waving to us as we sat on a bench with my dad. The day was cloudy and brisk, just on the cusp of a rain shower. We waved back.

Then she was gone.

By the time she passed, it had been a few years since my accident. I was used to bad dreams, or what I was told were bad dreams anyway, by this point. But some sort of burgeoning realization must have been brewing in my mind because, in addition to my usual nightly appeal, I added a line to my prayers: "Grandma, I love you but please don't come to see me."

I do recall being terrified that she would materialize before me. What's the old saying? I wish I knew then what I know now? I feel sad when I think about it, but I can't really fault my eight-year-old self. I was only a kid and it's probably best my beloved grandma didn't show up and end up categorized as just a bad dream.

That line remained in my prayers for over thirty years, until I finally decided it would be alright if she wanted to look in on me from time to time. However, she never has, that I know of.

I imagine, if you spend long enough pushing someone away, they may finally take the hint.

I'm sorry, grandma.

Perchance to Dream

I'm pretty sure that my mind started, at a very young age, to try and explain what was going on. My subconscious, however, often presents these messages to me in the form of dreams that resemble an Escher drawing.

The dreams my mother categorized as "bad" when I was a child soon morphed into recurring nightmares, but not necessarily the "monster in my closet" kind. Okay, one had a monster of sorts, but that was not the norm. These dreams tried, for many years, to tell me…something. I just wish I knew exactly what that something was.

I share them with you for two reasons. Firstly, I think you will find them entertaining. Secondly, I believe my dreams can be linked to the paranormal experiences I've had during my life. And so, here are my subconscious mind's greatest hits.

Heavy Footsteps

This dream lasted until I was around twenty-five years old.

I would go to sleep, and the scene would open on a beautiful, sunny day in New York City. I loved the city. I was born in the Bronx and spent many weekends with my parents roaming the canyons of Wall Street or on school trips to the museums in Manhattan. But after having this dream for so long, I knew the sunny day was about to transform. I would know what was coming but did not have the ability to stop it.

I've never been able to wake myself from a dream, so all I could do was let it play out each time.

In the dream, I'm walking down a busy street. Suddenly I become agitated and run into a tall office building. The lobby is quiet but, instead of taking the elevator, I head for the stairs and race up to the second floor. I push open the door and…

Everything is calm. People are quietly working at desks. Nobody looks my way.

I move back into the stairwell and run up to the next floor, throwing open that door to find a little more activity. People in work attire walking between desks, others looking at paperwork. But nothing out of the ordinary and nothing that would explain my disquiet.

The hum of office chatter begins to become audible, but I don't wait around. I'm back in the stairwell and up to the next floor, and the next, until I hit the sixth floor.

Tearing open that door, I am greeted with a visage of complete mayhem.

Papers fly in the wind, blowing through blown out floor-to-ceiling windows. People on this floor are running and screaming and trying to escape. But from what? I know, yet I don't know.

Then, I hear it. "Boom, boom, boom." Loud, thunderous footsteps, the footfalls rocking the building to its foundation.

Though my fear consumes me, I walk into the swirling vortex, glass crunching under my feet, and then I see it. A giant robot swaying past the gaping holes in the building. "Boom, boom, boom," back and forth he rocks. And I am terrified, but I can't escape, I can't wake up.

I back up against the inside wall of the office. Boom, boom, boom.

I look for a place to hide. Boom, boom, boom.

There's nowhere to go.

The massive automaton leans down and

peers through the gaping holes in the building. His huge eye looks right at me. I'm frozen in place.

Then I wake up, still hearing the booming sounds in my mind. It takes a few minutes for the fear to bleed off.

I hated this dream. When it finally ceased haunting me almost every night, I was grateful. I never figured out what it was trying to tell me.

Going Up?

This is another dream that dogged me for much of the first half of my life. This one, however, had a different outcome. As with the robot dream, I always knew when this one was about to begin.

In the dream, I open my eyes and I am at the end of a driveway or path that leads up to a multi-story building. Usually, it was a nondescript brick building although there were instances when it was a tall, glass-enclosed skyscraper. But for the most part, it was a brick building, its top floor visible making it about eight stories high, at the most. This, however, had no bearing on how the dream would play out. You will understand in a moment.

Walking up to the building, I would either enter through the front into the lobby or go around the back to a service entrance. Whichever way I chose, the goal was the same.

I was headed for the elevator.

Once at the lift, I press the call button and wait. There were two possible scenarios at this point. If I was at the service elevator, when its doors opened, the inside would be bare. The box would appear as if it were a poorly constructed tree house, wood planks for walls with bolts visible, barely holding it together or there would be moving blankets hung on the three inner walls.

If, however, the doors opened upon the elevator in the lobby, I would be greeted by what I can describe as a fully furnished, old-fashioned sitting room. There would be an overstuffed sofa with ball and claw feet, a floor lamp standing next to it with a disc shaped tabletop more than halfway down the pole, a coffee table set with a lovely doily, and an area rug to pull the whole room together. The lamp would be lit, casting a warm glow on what would be a most inviting setting, were it not the main player in my nightmare.

I don't remember ever sitting on the couch. Even in my addled subconscious mind, I realized the incongruity of what I was looking at or dreaming, as it were. I would just stand in front of the ill-placed room suite, facing the door. The other thing I don't recall is choosing a destination. The doors would close, and the box would begin to move even though I hadn't pressed a button to tell it where to go.

As an aside here, I would like to point

out something. If you enter an elevator, at least in New York City, and you do not push a button, the elevator will either ascend or descend to the next floor where someone else has called for it. In a multi-story building, there is usually someone waiting for or calling for an elevator. I make this point because it occurs to me that, in my dream, I never chose where I was going. The choice was being made for me by someone else. It only occurs to me now that this may have been significant and reminds me that hindsight is 20/20.

The elevator would begin to move normally. Up or down varied. Suddenly, it would jolt to a stop and before I could register the normal amount of aggravation and fear that arises when an elevator actually does that in real life, the box would begin to race in a sideways direction. Just as quickly, it would change direction as it picked up speed.

In the one elevator, I would be flung around along with the couch and lamp and throw rug. In the other, I would bounce from one wall to the other, hoping the shoddy workmanship that built it would not give way. Often, if I were in the service elevator, it would shrink around me until I felt as if I were being thrown about in a dumb waiter.

I remember the feeling of not knowing if I was going to crash through the walls or the roof of the building, fly through the air and plummet to earth.

The high-rise building version of the dream was even more harrowing. The building was always a glass covered leviathan and the elevator always closed in around me. I can't imagine what my sleeping heart rate must have been during these dreams because this building went higher than the clouds and the ride seemed to last forever before the dream would cease.

I would always awaken agitated and breathing hard, but very happy to not actually be on that carnival ride of a nightmare any longer. This dream haunted me for such a long time that I believed it would always be a part of me.

One night, when I was in my early thirties, married with my first child on the way, I went to bed and the dream began as usual. I walked up to the brick building, entered through the front door to the lobby, and called for the elevator. When the car arrived, I got in and the door closed. There was no furniture, and I did not feel the usual agitation.

This time, I hit a button for one of the floors. The elevator goes up. The elevator goes back down. The doors open, I walk out into the lobby and then out of the building. The dream ends and I never have it again. That was 30 years ago.

It only now occurs to me that the dream ended around the time of my marriage. If there is a deeper meaning there, I cannot say, but it sure is interesting, looking back.

Are There Messages In Dreams?

I do believe that many types of messages can come to us in our dreams if we are open to them. They can be our subconscious warning us about something going on in our daily life or they can be from those who have gone before us who are trying to help us navigate this crazy human existence.

I recall waking up one morning feeling euphoric. What I had dreamed the night before, I could not recall, however, I knew that everything and everyone I had ever known had been in that dream. The feeling lasted for three days, and I've often wished it would happen again.

As time went on, I started to question such a dream. Was it just that, or did I experience the sleeping equivalent of my life passing before my eyes?

Did I have a near death experience? I will never know. But I did have one prophetic dream that freaked me out so much, I had to call my mother.

A Snowy Premonition

I was single and living in an amazingly large studio apartment in White Plains, New York. My twenties were a very active time for me in a paranormal sense. I will share more on that later.

The winter Olympics of 1988 were taking place in Calgary, Canada and I enjoyed coming home each night to watch the day's competitions.

My brother was planning to fly out to visit a good friend in Arizona and they were planning to go up to Tahoe to do some skiing. A night or two before he was set to leave, I dreamt that he and his friend were skiing, one further down the hill, and a snow grooming machine drove between them and ran over one of them. I snapped awake, so upset, not just because of the dream itself, but because I hadn't seen which of them had been run over.

I called my mother as soon as I could,

the next morning, and told her of my dream. Mom has had her own lifetime of experiences and premonitions, so she calmed me down. We really couldn't do anything anyway. He was already on his way out west we agreed that he would make good decisions and be careful.

Most of us who have premonitions realize they may only be one version of what might come to pass. So, I left it to fate and my brother's good judgement.

As it turned out, I needn't have worried.

The next day, I came home and settled in to watch the days Olympic downhill skiing competitions. Before the event began, however, the announcer came on to let viewers know that the race had been cancelled for the day.

During the downtime between races, two skiers were descending the hill when they collided, and a snow cat ran over one of them.

This also demonstrates the futility of experiencing premonitions. You can't know for sure who the message is for, and even if you think you do, nobody will believe you anyway.

Voices on the Wind

This is one of the most profound paranormal experiences I have had throughout my life. It began when I was around sixteen years old. We had just moved to a new house, and I was thrilled because I did not have to go back to my old high school, a place where I had no friends and was bullied quite a lot.

My parents' bedroom was at one end of the upstairs hall and we three kids' rooms were at the opposite end. I was in the middle. It started one night. I was lying in bed and either still awake or was awakened by a female voice calling to me.

My first name is Cynthia and I've never thought of myself as a Cindy. Only my closest family and friends call me Cindy and those are the people that I respond to when I hear it. If anyone else calls me by that name, I don't even turn around.

But in the dark of the night, a female voice would begin to call to me in a singsong manner, "Ciiiiindy" usually three times, "Ciiiindy, Ciiiindy", the tone increasing with each utterance of the name. I would pull the covers up to my face and try to hide, hoping that whomever the voice belonged to would not come through my door.

There were times I was so frightened I would call out to my parents loudly, their bedroom about thirty feet away.

I would call out "MOM? DAD? Is that YOU?" This would result in my father angrily yelling at me to go back to sleep because he had to go to work in the morning.

I detested hearing this voice call to me in the dark. Then, it began to happen during the day. I could be outside or even at the mall.

I know that sounds strange. If you are at such a place, with people all around, the odds of hearing people call each other are high. Of course, someone might be calling someone else in my vicinity named Cindy. That goes without saying.

But there was something about the voice, and the feeling I had when it would happen, something that would become more prevalent later in my life.

I now call it the "cone of silence" (nod to Get Smart) and that's what it feels like. I feel as if I am in a bubble and I can feel pressure in my ears, as if I am in a vacuum that allows the voice to pierce through while muting everything else around me.

These were not fun experiences and I never felt that I could share them with anyone lest I be thought mentally incompetent. Honestly, I wondered about this myself at times.

When I went to college, this was the one experience that followed me. Granted, I was rarely alone during those years, having a roommate the first two semesters and living in a house with fifty-two other women for the rest of my time at university.

It wasn't until after I'd graduated that I found a kindred spirit. While I was having a conversation with one of my best college chums, she admitted to having the same experiences during her teen years.

When I finished college, I moved home to live with my mother. At this point, my parents were no longer together. I moved back into my old room, now painted a lovely, light color, and I no longer experienced my name being called from the ether.

Evolution of The Shadow Man

I went to college for five years. Sometimes, it takes a little longer than the average four. Unfortunately, dropping classes early on because you're a Journalism major who hates math but still ends up a member of MENSA catches up with you eventually. The result was having to get an apartment with a friend and take an additional year's worth of classes.

That got cut short thanks to a screwed-up diagnosis by a DO (as in not an MD). I moved home in 1983 and finished my last few credits at a local community college. Luckily, I was still able to get my degree from my university. The abrupt transfer back to my old teenage bedroom, however, hastened the beginning of the next paranormal chapter of my life.

Before I went away, I loved to sleep in the sensory deprivation chamber that was my bedroom, the walls painted the darkest blue.

Except for occasionally hearing my name called by some disembodied voice, it was perfect, and I used to sleep soundly.

Fast forward four and half years. I moved home and the room had been repainted a lovely, light color that I can't even recall. I was surprised because in all the time I was at school, she never mentioned the change. But I didn't think that much of it. During those years my parents had gotten divorced and I'm sure the thought of selling the house had a lot to do with the choice. Apparently, most home buyers aren't thrilled when they see a room painted almost black. While there are probably many families who might appreciate the Addams Family vibe, I can understand my mother not wanting to deal with the issue.

I made the drive back home with my dad. He was forced to horseshoe himself into the bright yellow Volkswagen bug I bought when I traded in the Camaro he had bought for me. He was not happy about the trade or the ride, but we made it back from Iowa in two days. I don't think he ever rode in that car again.

It felt odd to be back home in New York. I had toyed with the idea of staying out west and had even interviewed for a job in Chicago at one point, having lived there one summer. But I am pretty sure I'm a New York City snob and felt the east coast was the only place to be. So, I signed up for my classes and my aunt got me a job at her cable company in customer service.

At this point, it had been a while since I had any paranormal experiences, so I was relaxed and ready to get on with getting on with my life. I finished school and ended up with a job in the city at an ad agency. Nothing terribly exciting. I was an executive secretary for one of the big shots. That lasted about a year before I got a similar job at CBS, right across from the building they call Blackrock, in the city. The commute was hell from where I lived, the old trains basically torture devices, too cold in the winter and blisteringly hot in the summer. I was up at six a.m. so I could catch the seven o'clock train and often not home until seven thirty or eight p.m. most nights, the ride an hour and forty-five grueling minutes each way.

My bed faced a large closet with two wooden sliding doors and the door to the room, to the left of that. With the new, lighter paint scheme, on all but the darkest, moonless nights, I could still open my eyes in the dark and see an outline of both.

One night, after I had settled in, I awoke. I knew it was the middle of the night but didn't hear any noise that might have been the cause of my waking. I do remember the old fear of waiting to hear my name called and I lay there looking at the ceiling, hoping it would not happen. It didn't, but my relief was short lived.

Certain that I was not going to be beckoned from beyond, I relaxed, and my eyes traveled down from the ceiling to the closet wall.

Standing in front of my closet was the outline of a shadowy figure, a man, wearing a bowler hat. The entire figure was black with no apparent features that I could discern but, somehow, I knew it was a man. Who it was, I still couldn't say as I didn't know any British folks at the time.

I was, however, startled. This was the first time I had ever experienced seeing anything like this. I remember just staring at the figure, waiting for it to move, or speak, or something. But it did none of those things. Not knowing what I should do, I slowly reached for my lamp and flicked it on. Once the room was illuminated, of course, he was gone.

I was stunned by what had just occurred but hoped it was just a one-time occurrence.

It wasn't.

I can't remember now if it happened every night, but it was certainly way too often for my liking, and, as time went on, I would wake to find the shadow man closer and closer to my bed. Eventually, he was standing at the foot of my bed, yet his figure was still a bottomless, black void, shaped like a bowler-wearing gentleman.

This visitor made no sense to me. I'd never known anyone personally who wore a bowler, a hat popular in the United Kingdom. My relatives came from the Bronx and, in their hay day, wore fedoras. No comparison.

I would have to say this went on for the better part of a year. Then, one night when I awoke, he was gone. No shadow man. Just my room and the maw of my closet doors in the dark.

I was so relieved that this might finally be over. Even now, thirty-six years later, I can remember the feeling washing over me. I could finally go to sleep and not wonder if he would be there, watching me. It was wonderful.

So, I rolled to my right side. And I screamed and jumped the other way, clear off the bed.

Kneeling next to my bed was a man, a big man wearing khaki pants and a short sleeved, buttoned-down cotton shirt. He had dark hair and a close beard, and dark eyes. And he was pointing right at me with his right index finger.

I could not get the lights on fast enough. Once I did, he was gone. Fear had rushed through me like a chill blast of wind, and it took me a few minutes to slow my breathing.

When I remember back to that moment,

and all those that followed, I can still feel the blood pulsing at my temples. I was terrified. He was as real to me as you might be if you were standing, or kneeling, next to me.

I had no idea who he was. I still don't but, all these years later, if I had an ounce of artistic ability in my bones, I could draw you a picture of him. His face and his entire body are imprinted in my mind. I can still see him.

But who was he and why was he pointing at me? I still don't know, but he plagued me for the next five years.

When I moved into my own apartment, he came along.

Sometimes you Conduit, and sometimes you con't...

I moved into my own apartment, a huge studio on the fifth floor of a six-floor building. The owner was a client of my new boss and I got a heck of a great deal. It was 1985 and my rent was $325 a month. I loved it.

In the winter, I could walk around in shorts in the place, my windows cracked open. The landlord would always pump the heat up so it would make it to the sixth floor, "for the old folks" he would tell me.

Unfortunately, kneeling pointing man like the place as well. I can't remember how often I would wake up to him next to my bed.

But some more interesting things began to happen as well.

This was my twenties, and it became the most active time in my life, as far as my paranormal experiences. And the most negative. Kneeling man was one thing, but there was so much more.

I had a boyfriend at the time who would stay over. One morning, he told me that I had woken up, sat up, and told him my mother and my natural mother were standing at the end of the bed. Then, I lay down and went back to sleep.

The next day, I called my mother and asked if I'd been adopted. She didn't appreciate the question.

I tell you this because, while I don't remember what I saw that night, I did have many other instances where I woke up to something, or someone, standing and watching me.

Very often, I would wake up while sleeping on my sleeper couch in the living room, look over and see a shadow person standing in my kitchen. Not the same one as at my house. No bowler hat. Just a person, a man. In my kitchen.

One of my more memorable experiences was waking to see a woman wearing a prison dress with one arm crossed in front of her. It stood out because she was headless. I can still see her when I close my eyes. Some things stick with you.

Evil Whispers

This is one of my more unenjoyable experiences. It was actually a series of unenjoyable experiences that lasted for quite some time.

There were times when I thought I was losing my mind. My inner mantra was that I was going to end up going to either a psychic or a psychiatrist. This next series of experiences put me over the edge and pushed me to finally seek out one of the two.

As if the kneeling man experience wasn't bad enough, I began to experience the sensation of waking up with someone sitting or lying next to me in the dark. I don't mean my boyfriend. This only happened when I was alone.

It terrified me every time it happened. I would awaken in the dark and freeze, sensing I was not alone.

Then, whatever it was would whisper in my ear. I could feel their breath on me. They would say two words to me, only two words, not always the same. They would darkly whisper:

"I'm insane." Or

"I'm crazy" or

"I'm disturbed"

It was so frightening that all I could do each time was slowly reach for the light switch and get the lights on as quickly as possible.

In one instance, I was staying at my father's ski condo. He was sleeping upstairs, and I was in a low loft above the living room. It was so low, you could not stand but, luckily, the light consisted of a bulb with a hanging string right above my head.

When I was awoken and felt the presence next to me, even in my terrified state, I was able to reach up and turn on the light. It felt like I reached forever. I truly believed every time that I would turn on the light and find someone there.

Thankfully, I never did because the picture my mind's eye drew of whoever it was that would have been there was horrifying.

Terrors in the Night (and sometimes the Day)

No, that's not the name of an Opus by Beethoven. It's a sleep disorder, commonly referred to as "night terrors", that I've dealt with for over thirty years. After all this talk about dreams, I thought I'd share this with you.

Night Terrors, however, are not dreams at all.

The Oxford dictionary is plain and to the point. It is "a sleep terror disorder. Also called night terrors (From Latin "pavor" – fear or dread plus "nocturnus" – of the night)." I could go into the scientific or medical information, such as the fact that this affliction mostly affects children and only 2.2% of adults[2], or that it occurs during the early sleep stages of non-REM sleep. But in the context of this book, I mainly want to share my own experience with it. I do this because it is an intrinsic part of who I am, and this book both serves the purpose of sharing with you my lifetime of paranormal experiences as well as documenting for my posterity many of my own idiosyncrasies, not the least of which is my perceived ability to communicate with the other side.

That was a long sentence. I apologize.

Another reason for sharing this information with you is that, in an upcoming

---

[2] https://www.sleepfoundation.org/night-terrors

chapter, I will describe some of my paranormal experiences. Many of them have occurred at night yet I have never confused a night terror episode with one of them. You will understand why this makes sense very shortly.

What Did He Get Himself Into?

I don't recall experiencing night terrors when I was single. Mostly, I was having nightly visits from various ghostly wanderers. The first time it happened was after I was married.

My poor husband. The man is a saint. He's never said it but I'm sure he's asked himself who, or what, he married. Let me tell you about the incidents that stand out in both our memories, the ones he likes to tell people about at parties. It's a great conversation starter, evidently.

I was eight and a half months pregnant with my daughter. As my husband tells it, in what seemed like the middle of the night, he heard me yell "get down! Get down!". When he opened his eyes, I was standing on the bed, but not for long. He says I leapt off the bed onto the floor and began yelling and beckoning him to join me, saying the same thing again, until he shouted my name, and I awoke.

I gained a good deal of weight when I was pregnant. It must have been quite a sight to behold. He said he feared for the life of our unborn child because I dove stomach first from the bed.

My daughter is fine. She's now thirty years old and suffered no ill effects from that night.

Night terrors are not the result of a dream or a nightmare. They happen in an instant. The only memory I have from that instance is that, in that fraction of a second, I saw the tip of an imaginary rifle peak through our curtains. I remember telling him that the next day and telling him how real it felt. I remember the feeling of my heart beating a tattoo in my chest, but that happened every time so it may be a general memory that I connect with every terror I experienced. It happened many times. This one still stands out as one of the more impressive.

Here's another one. My husband and I work together. We have for over twenty years. One day at work I noticed that he wasn't saying much to me. He seemed miffed about something, but I had no idea what that something was. Finally, I asked him what was up.

His reply was "Don't you remember what you did last night?"

I do remember feeling dumbfounded and stating that I had no idea what he was talking about.

He told me that I had sat up in bed and

punched him in the face. Then I lay back down and went right back to sleep.

I was gob smacked. I realize that, in retrospect, it seems funny and makes for good story telling. But at the time, I felt terrible. At first, I couldn't believe it. How does a person punch another person, their spouse for goodness' sake, in the FACE, and not remember it?

In addition, he seemed genuinely hurt by it. I simply couldn't fathom what on earth was wrong with my subconscious mind.

You do remember I said that my husband is a saint? It's not just for putting up with me. The man, in no way, deserved being socked in the mouth by his sleeping wife.

All I could do was apologize. I wracked my brain trying to remember any bit of it. But like the night terror it was, it happened in a flash, and in a flash, it was gone, leaving no record in the available RAM of my brain. I often wonder where in the gray folds of my hippocampus that bit of memory resides.

Most of my night terrors went like this: We're sleeping soundly when suddenly I jump up, yelling (I don't scream, even on roller coasters), and run from the bedroom, through the house, turning on lights as I go until I reach the front of the house. I wake up, my heart pounding and adrenalin rushing through my body. I have no idea why I'm there. All I can feel is fear fading from my system. But fear of what? I have no idea. I turn off the lights one by one on the way back to bed. My husband, who is a light sleeper, asks me if I'm alright. He always asks, "What happened?" and I never have much of an answer.

One night, I jumped up, hauled off and punched the wall. Like a prize fighter. I woke up immediately. It hurt like hell.

And then there was the one and only time I ran completely through the house, turning on lights, as I headed to the kitchen, and grabbed a steak knife out of the cutlery drawer.

Thankfully, I immediately woke up, knife in hand. It was disconcerting, to say the least and it's never happened since. But, whenever someone asks us if night terrors are dangerous, we just look at each other, and then he tells the story.

On a serious note, if you have sleep issues that are affecting your waking hours or concerning you, speak to your doctor. There are sleep studies that can be done to determine a root cause and possibly some way to mitigate the situation.

I have found that my night terrors have occurred during times of stress, a common culprit in many maladies that afflict people. Whatever the cause, don't suffer. Seek assistance.

Déjà vu All Over Again

I hate déjà vu.

It's a French phrase that simply means "already seen" and I have experienced it a number of times during my life, as has my daughter. Modern medicine eschews any correlation between déjà vu and the paranormal, and the research I have read certainly makes all the sense in the world to me.

I bring it up because it is an experience I cannot explain, much like my paranormal experiences. In the context of my life, I consider it part of my journey.

One interesting fact is that my instances

of déjà vu have affected me in a totally different way than my paranormal experiences. The discomfort that has resulted from them was at a level that I can still recall, viscerally. They've taken my breath away.

If you've ever had a similar experience, you will understand. The sensation comes over you, unexpectedly, and you freeze as you try to process what you are seeing, because you swear you've been there before in that exact moment and place. It's not like you've visited the spot before. You have lived this moment already. Your mind takes a stutter step, and you feel like a reel of old eight-millimeter film stuck in the projector.

One instance that stands out is my first

day at my first job after college. I studied Journalism and thought I'd become a magazine writer one day. So, naturally, I took a job as an executive secretary to the Vice President at an ad agency in New York City. I could type one hundred thirteen words per minute, which didn't hurt.

The offices of Avrett, Free and Ginsburg were on Second Avenue, if memory serves. I remember the great Indian food on Third Avenue at lunchtime and the Mulligatawny soup.

The train ride in and out of the city was torture most days. Then, I had to walk from 42nd Street to the office and I hated seeing women wearing suits and sneakers, so I ruined many a pair of high heels because of my vanity.

I also spent far too much time at Saks Fifth Avenue on my lunch breaks.

When I was interviewed, it was in a meeting room, and I did not see my workstation. Another employee escorted me to my desk that first morning. We walked down a long hallway, away from the chatter of the art rooms and other offices and came upon an open work area with a desk and all manner of office accoutrements. The desk backed up to an almost floor to ceiling window with the most magnificent view of the city. Walled on three sides, the area was private and tucked away from the rest of the office. My new boss' office door was on the right.

As I walked to the desk, a sudden sense

of déjà vu hit me. I felt that, undeniably, I had experienced this moment already.

It's hard to explain if you haven't felt it. Even if I had possibly glanced down this long hall at some point during the interview process, I knew that was not what I was feeling. This moment, somewhere, somehow, in my mind, had already occurred.

It left an impression, because still, all these years later, I can recall the feeling. And that was 1984, forty years ago.

My Daughter's Ground Hog Days

My thirty-year-old daughter shared some of her experiences with me.

One such time was when she was in high school. She woke in the morning, went to school, and was halfway through her day when she suddenly woke up in her bed. It became doubly disconcerting when, after getting over the initial shock, she arose, went to school, and the day played out just as she had already experienced.

On another occasion, she dreamt that I spoke to her upon her waking one day and let her know that her friend had called to invite her to a strawberry festival. She said that, in her dream, she was apprehensive but ended up going to the festival. At one point while there, she came upon a couple sitting at the food court and remembered being "freaked out" upon seeing them for some unknown reason.

When she awoke from her dream, I was at her bedroom door letting her know that her friend had called to invite her to the festival. As the day began to play out exactly as in her dream, she came upon those same people, a bald man and his wife, in the food area of the festival, and she freaked out because she had remembered them from her dream.

The odd thing was, in her dream, before she had ever gone to the festival, she remembered her reaction to the couple, whom she had never met before. Why did she react that way in the dream before the day had occurred?

We have discussed this and all we can

come up with is that the dream was not the first time she had experienced that day. It's a brain twister, for sure.

If You have Ghosts…

I drive my daughter crazy.

The girl walks silent, on little cat feet, and has a habit of walking into a room when my back is turned, or when I'm on the computer wearing headphones. Countless times, I've sensed her presence and turned to find her looking at me, sheepishly, as she apologizes for her seemingly sneaky entrance. She doesn't do it on purpose, and she's always amazed when I don't react.

It's very difficult to "jump scare" me. The reason: I always take for granted there's someone there. I know that may sound a tad manic, and I'm not saying I'm surrounded by spirits all the time. I'm saying we all are.

I remember a conversation with friends, talking about walking around our houses at night, especially if nobody else is home. My honest response was that I had no issue with it at all. They found this surprising, most of them sharing that it scared them and that they refused to do it. To me, that made no sense. Firstly, it's my house, so why would it? And second, again, they're always there anyway.

Half the time, I walk around my house in the dark with my eyes closed, anyway.

Let me explain. I became a EMT in 1998 and was a member of a firehouse that required I be an exterior firefighter as well. To do this, I was enrolled in courses at the fire training center, Firefighter 1 and Intermediate. I was issued a full set of gear, which included turnout gear, helmet, and a Nomex hood. The hood is a fire-retardant balaclava and is worn over the head and under the helmet. It overlaps with the breathing mask, which hooks to the air tank. These are worn when entering a fire building, something I did get to do during training.

It was very exhilarating, going into the three-story, block, structure made to mimic a small multi-family apartment building. The bottom floor was set ablaze, and I can still feel the heat of the flames on my face. You'd think you wouldn't feel it through the mask and all that gear, but you do. Floor to ceiling, roaring flames.

We practiced on the nozzle and learned that you hit the fire in a clockwise motion, not the other way around. The theory is a counterclockwise circle will draw the fire to you.

Floor to ceiling, floor to ceiling, you hit the fire until it hopefully goes out. You're in a crouch, and the other firefighters are snug up against you and each other, hanging onto the hose. Push enough water through and it can take three of you to keep it from becoming a humiliating carnival ride.

It's hot, hotter than you realize until you are face to face with it. And you learn. That gear is flame retardant, not fireproof. It gives you time. It doesn't make you bulletproof.

We also practiced going out the third story window. You learn how to get out in a hurry. It was fun. Of course, there are very few buildings that tall in my town, so hopefully I'll never have to go out a third story window again.

There was one other major type of training we did, which brings me back to my original point about walking around my house with my eyes closed. It was called "mask confidence". This is the one that freaks out a lot of people, especially if they are claustrophobic. If you're claustrophobic, you probably won't want to try this. You also probably don't want to become an interior firefighter.

The idea behind running the mask confidence course is to become comfortable with moving around a building or house when you can't see. When there is a fire situation, firefighters' first objective is to preserve life, and this involves searching for potential victims before concentrating on fighting the fire. There might be no power at night in a darkened basement but more than likely we're talking about smoke.

You can't see through smoke.

Training for this situation is two-fold.

First, we learn and practice specific methods of searching: the right-hand search and the left-hand search. Basically, we go in on our knees, one behind the other, and maintain contact with the person in front of us while sticking to the left- or right-hand wall. Searching is done with your outside hand and whatever tool you brought in, usually a Halligan bar. The Halligan is the go-to tool of firefighters. It's a crowbar on one end and an adze and pick on the other. It's very handy for going through doors or windows, both forcefully and for "sounding". Hitting the floor on the other side.

If you go through a door or a window, you "sound" the floor on the other side first, because sometimes it's not there anymore.

My training is done, mostly, without the smoke and without the fire. So how do we simulate the blackout environment of a smoke-filled structure?

You turn your Nomex hood around.

The mask confidence course we had to take was in a separate structure at the training center. Basically, we started fully geared with our hoods on backwards, mask on and air tank on our backs. We entered the course blind and on our knees. The night I went through, we were running late, so I ended up lead with a guy behind me. At one point, there was a window. I know it was a window and I was sure to sound the floor on the other side before hefting my leg up and going through.

The most challenging part of the course was a hole in the floor that we had to enter. I could hear the proctor skitter across the floor above us as he followed our progress. We had to remove our SCBA air tanks and push them ahead of us, without losing the regulator that fed us air.

It was exhilarating and I was very proud of myself for completing the course, especially since the guy that went in with me got a little hinky when we were under the floor. He was desperate not to lose hold of my gear and kept pulling on me as I inched forward. I could tell by his pissy tone that he was not happy to be under a floorboard in this confined space. I still wonder if he continued his training.

That was twenty years ago. I still have my certificate though I'm no longer an EMT/firefighter. I am, however, glad I did it and proud of my fifteen years of service.

That seemed like a roundabout way to explain why I walk around my house in the dark with my eyes closed, but it is the reason. That training made me realize this: If I try to feel my way around in the dark with my eyes open, I will still be trying to "see". My brain, through the windows of my eyes, will still be searching for anything to anchor me. But if I close my eyes, and my other senses take over, I find my way just fine.

Why was I telling you all this anyway? I honestly don't remember. This chapter is really about the spirit visitations I've had throughout my life, how they have changed, and how I experience it now. So, let's talk about that.

Who Are You Gonna Call?

I've already written about my twenties and what a cornucopia of spirit "contact" I experienced. The parentheses are there because I don't consider all those experiences true spirit contact. Not in the sense that I do now, anyway.

During that decade of my life, I thought I would be driven mad by all of it. My mantra was "I either need a psychic or a shrink." No offense was meant towards anyone in that field of healthcare. It's just something I shared with friends or said to myself often.

At the point when my ethereal visitations became an almost nightly endeavor, I decided that I would visit a psychic for some advice. It was easier and less costly than going to a psychiatrist.

It's too long ago now. I can't even remember how I found the woman or what her name was, but she ended up being an immeasurable help to me, then and ever since. I'm sure the story of my session with her will sound like so many others, but I'm going to share it with you anyway.

She told me that I am an old soul. She also told me that, because of my "gift" and because I had no idea how to control it, I was being used as a conduit by myriad spirits to come through.

I had no idea what their reasons for pushing through the veil were because none of them ever spoke to me. Not the pointing man crouching next to my bed, not the headless woman. Well, she may have had a hard time, not having a mouth, or a head. The shadow man standing in my kitchen just stood there, and the malevolent entity that would whisper horrible things in my ear was probably not an entity I would have wanted to have a long conversation with anyway.

It's very possible that, because I was so afraid back then, I never gave them the chance to communicate with me. Now, looking back,

I'd love to know why they were there, and if I could have helped them in any way.

What the psychic taught me was that I had the power to control the contact. I could close the door, block the path. It was my choice to either let them through or not. This had never occurred to me. When something starts so early in your life, you feel as if it's a part of you that you can't change.

She also showed me that the power of good will always win out over the powers of evil. It took me a little while to get it under control, but not long after I finally had peace at night.

Pax et Quietam

Then I got married.

The next few years were blissfully quiet. I had a new roommate, and we subsequently had a couple of kids. It was a busy time. We bought a house and a couple of years later, in 1993, sold that house and lived with my in-laws for ten months. There was very little alone time. We lived in the basement which we totally fitted out for our little family. In the winter, as a side gig, my husband became Mr. Plow. I would ride along with him from driveway to driveway while the family watched my daughter and did all the invoicing using a rudimentary computer program, we bought for ten dollars.

We finally decided to buy a condo because, as gracious as his parents were to let us live with them, it was time for us to be on our own again. If you've ever lived with your mother and father in-law, you know from whence I speak.

They are both gone now, and I miss them terribly. They should be here.

Speaking of Family: Mom

My parents divorced while I was away at college. It was for the best, really, but everything leading up to it was tough.

My mom remarried a couple of years later and was over the moon happy but, sadly, her second husband passed away a year later.

We were all devastated. Bill was a man's man and he had helped my youngest brother get back on track in school and in his life after he had suffered first-hand the last tumultuous years of my parent's marriage while I was away at college.

Sadly, a severe allergic reaction to medication, something Bill had rarely taken during his life, caused irreversible brain damage. It took him a year to die, my mother caring for him every moment.

After Bill became ill, mom had to take him to a doctor after hours in New Rochelle.

She had to park in an alley and get him up to the doctor's office through the back door. It was winter and icy outside. When they went back to the car, she had to get him out of his wheelchair and into the back seat. As she lifted him, she slipped on the ice and knew they were both going to fall as Bill could not do anything to help himself. She cried out "God, please help me" as she felt herself going down and suddenly there was a man behind her, asking to help. He did and they did not fall. He was able to help her get Bill into the car, and he even folded up the wheelchair. When my mother turned to thank him, he was gone.

Another time, mom was sitting at a red light. When the light turned green, and just before she was going to press the gas pedal, she heard my dad's voice (her ex-husband) say "Don't Go!" She hesitated and just then another vehicle came barreling through the intersection across the front of her vehicle, and through the red light. Had she not heeded the message, she would have been killed.

My mother has a psychic connection with both her sister and one of her best friends. She will receive messages that tell her something is up with either of them and will then call to find out what is wrong. It's a two-way street as they do the same with her.

About a week after Bill passed, my mom was lying on her bed taking an afternoon rest when she heard the jingling of keys and looked up from the bed in what was their master bedroom. She saw Bill and watched as he placed his big ring of keys and pocket change into the dish on the dresser, the way he always did at the end of a long workday.

She can still vividly recall her elation and wonderment as he smiled at her. Without saying a word, she knew he was alright, and that he'd come to check up on her. And then he was gone. That was 1986. She recounts his visitation to this day, her story never wavering.

Little did I know that, thirty-three years later, Bill would come through during one of my sessions. But I'm getting ahead of myself. I'll share that story with you in another chapter. Let me tell you about my spirit contact now. There is a world of difference from those harrowing years before I controlled the door to this side.

My mother shared one final story with me about her Bill. A year and a half before his passing, they were getting ready to go out to dinner. They were happy, with no signs of what was to come.

My mother stopped in the bathroom just before they left. While she was there, she had a vision. It was of a gray, overcast day, with light rain falling. She was riding in a limousine, and someone was sitting beside her. When she looked out to one side of the car, the street was lined with firefighters. Out the other side of the road, she saw police officers. Bill was the chief of police, and my mother realized it was his funeral she was seeing. She says she chided herself for having such a terrible thought and put it out of her mind. Eighteen months later, she found herself in that limo. It was a gray, overcast day, with light rain falling. My Aunt Johanna was sitting next to her as they rode through town for Bill's last patrol.

There are two ways that I experience direct spirit contact these days. The first are the random nighttime visitations. Yes, I still have them, but these do not frighten me any longer. It seems that I have universal control over what enters my psychic personal space, even when sleeping.

One of my most recent incidents was quite humorous. I found it funny, even at the time. I'd been asleep in bed and awoke in the middle of the night for no apparent reason. The room was pitch black, as usual, my husband and I preferring to sleep with no light whatsoever. The only faint light, a small, blue, glows from on top of the wireless internet connection.

As my eyes adjusted, I realized that a young man was crawling, rapidly, across the bed in front of me. He stopped short and we stared at each other. He was wearing swimming trunks and was bare chested, and he had wavy short hair that tumbled around his head.

His smile was wide and as I began to speak, he completed his traverse of the bed, and was gone.

I looked over at my husband who was

still fast asleep. He sleeps with a pillow over his head, so even my sitting up didn't disturb him. The room was silent once more and so I lay back down and eventually went back to sleep.

I can still see the young man's smile in my mind's eye. I hope he had a good swim.

Another recent incident, I believe, has its roots in another that occurred a few years ago. About five years ago, my son had a friend from college stay over and we set him up out back in the family room on the pullout couch. Now, we've lived in our house for twenty years at this point, and the only ghostly visitor we can all agree upon is one black cat that likes to slink around and then vanish. It's been seen by everyone in the family, and by a few visitors as well.

We were very surprised when my son came to us after his friend had left the next day. He said the friend had told him that his house was haunted. When my son asked what he meant, the young man told him of the shadow figure that had scared him the night before.

This was the first we had ever heard of such a presence in our home. That fellow never visited us again.

About two years later, my son was in Oklahoma with his then-girlfriend for a family wedding (her family). One night, he called me, and he was whispering but I could tell he was very upset. He had been given a couch to sleep on in the living room of a rental house and everyone else was asleep. Evidently, he could see down a hallway and, while he lay on the couch playing on his phone, a shadow figure peered around a door jam, stared right at him, and then withdrew back into a room.

My son was beside himself and wanted to know how this could happen, why it would happen, and what he could do to make it never happen again. I really felt terrible for him and all those feelings from my younger days came flooding back. The fear, the frustration, the hating my "gift".

We've had numerous conversations about it since, and all I can do is share with him what I've learned over the years.

Fast forward to last year. I was speaking

to my daughter in our back family room, the same room where my son's friend had slept. I had my back to the hallway, and she stood facing me. As we were discussing something, she suddenly looked over my shoulder as if to say hello to someone but then a look of confusion came over her face and she told me to hang on a minute.

She walked past me into the hallway and called out to her father, because she was sure she'd just seen him down the hall.

When I told her he wasn't even home, I could see her bristle. She'd seen a man, and just figured it was him. We both went forward into the house, cautiously, now not sure if someone else had gotten in without us knowing. But there was nobody there.

The second incident, I believe, relates to these. Again, I was lying in bed, not yet asleep for the evening. My husband was already out, and I suddenly sensed a presence. I did not sit up but as I looked up toward the dim light of the internet beacon, I could see it.

A very tall figure in shadow stood at the end of my bed. It is possible it was floating because, if it were standing, that would mean it was almost eight feet tall. I could see the outline and I thought "how classic". The figure was hooded with no discernible features. Granted, the room was very dark, but I sensed the lack of facial features more than saw.

I stared for a minute, and moved my

head to the right and left, trying to convince myself it was not there, that it was a reflection. But there is just not enough light in the room at night to cause such a reflection. So, I resigned myself to it being there.

At that point, I simply said "okay, what do you need?" to which I did not receive any reply. Just a silent stare from non-existent eyes. To be honest, I wasn't all that happy as I was tired and just wanted to go to sleep. Receiving no reply after asking again, that is exactly what I did.

The second way I have spirit contact is something that happens much more rarely but, when it does, it is significant and undeniable. I call it the Cone of Silence.

The sensation I am referring to began when I was a teenager and would hear my name called at night or in public places. Before that happened, I would feel the sensation around me as if I were suddenly in a vacuum. Sound around me would diminish and become muffled. This was my sign that something was about to happen.

The last time this happened was during a difficult time when my husband was trying to work with his sisters to take care of his widowed father. I was sitting at my computer when I felt pressure in my ears and the cone descended around me.

When I have spirit contact, I see the

spirit, however it's as if they are standing right behind me. In this instance, my late mother-in-law was just off my right shoulder.

I will tell you that I have a spirit guide that I call David, as I believe he has told me that is his name in sessions I have held. He is an older man, very thin, with shoulder length gray hair. He wears khaki pants and a short sleeved, button down, light cotton shirt and when I see him, he is always smiling. This is how I know everything is alright.

So, David is behind me, off my left shoulder, and my mother-in-law is off my right. She's there because she's concerned about my father-in-law and I know what her message is. She knows my son will take care of him and she wants to make sure he does.

There had been some back and forth with the sisters about them possibly taking over and moving him closer to where they live, but after this visit, I knew that he was safest remaining right near us.

Not long after, I attended a bridal shower with my two sisters in law and shared with the older of the two what had happened. I was cautious, but her eyes opened wide, and she was adamant that she believed me and wanted to heed her mother's advice.

The author at Burnside Bridge, Antietam

Dr. Ray, Digital EVP session at

Bonaventure Cemetery, Savannah, Ga.

Old grave, Hilton Head Isl, S.Carolina

Letchworth Village, Thiells, New York

Letchworth Village, abandoned hospital

Wall Gravestones, Savannah, Ga.

Forgotten roadside cemetery, Auburn, NY

Sleepy Hollow Cemetery, NY

Gettysburg, Pennsylvania Battlefield

Colonial Park Cemetery, Savannah

What is ITC?

"The day science begins to study non-physical phenomena, it will make more progress in one decade than in all the previous centuries of its existence."
— **Nikola Tesla**

I never thought of my experiences with the spirit world as paranormal.

To me, they were my normal, my baseline. The word "paranormal" wasn't normalized until I was in my forties and I'm pretty sure that was due to the advent of televised ghost hunting entertainment. I won't say the names of the shows, but one of them was synonymous with Sprit Frolic.

That one program opened the flood

gates, and I can't even count how many others have come on the scene since. But for me, and others like me, up until then, our experiences were more akin to "he who shall not be named." They weren't popular or exciting, and sharing them could result in harsh side-glances or party guests making bathroom excuses and backing away awkwardly.

I severely limited who I shared my "gift" with for most of my life. When, suddenly, a national audience was created and terms such as "paranormal investigator" and "spirit contact" became part of the lexicon, I felt as if a weight had been lifted.

Of course, I didn't run out and shout from the rooftops, "Hey! I do talk to dead people!". If the subject was broached in conversation or at a gathering, my first reaction would still be to demure and try to change the subject. Now though, once those I'm speaking with realize my history and my current involvement in the paranormal, conversations seem to take a very unexpected turn.

None of the negativity I had always expected surfaces. Sure, there are people that will tell me they do not believe in the ability to speak to those who are not here with us in corporeal form, and I'm good with that. But, for the most part, I find that folks are intensely interested in what I do, what I know, and what might be. It's quite refreshing to finally be able to talk about it, after all these years.

So, what is ITC? It's an acronym for Instrumental Trans-communication and it refers to the theory that we can use instruments, such as radios or recorders, to communicate with those in the spirit realm. It is the testing of this theory that is the basis for all the ghost box and EVP sessions I do on my YouTube channel and it's something I discovered about five years ago.

I'm not sure how I came across them, but I came to discover a community of people using "hacked" radios to do just what this theory promotes. I'd never seen the like of it and watched many sessions by these self-proclaimed investigators. They ran the gamut from one person in their kitchen to large teams with matching t-shirts and corporate sponsors.

I was excited as I watched these folks and decided to give it a try. After a lifetime of unbidden spirit contact that I could never actually show to another person, I was enthralled with the concept of recording my experiences and having some tangible "proof" to finally share with other people.

So, I bought a ghost box.

Tesla Talked to Aliens

Nikola Tesla was a genius. He was an electrical engineer and a physicist who lived from 1856 to 1943. Among his inventions are alternating current (AC), wireless communication, and the rotating magnetic field electric motor.

In the paranormal community, Tesla is heralded as one of its forefathers. There are a couple of reasons for this.

When he was seven years old, Nikola Tesla, the son and grandson of Serbian Orthodox priests, witnessed the death of his older brother, Dane, in a riding accident. Some accounts opine that Nikola caused the accident by spooking the horse.

After the accident, he began seeing visions which he described as "flames in the air". [3] He claimed he could control them using willpower. He also claimed, much later in his life, that he could communicate with the New York City pigeons using the same power.

In 1899, he believed he had intercepted messages from "another world". Though these were a series of out of place beeps heard through a radio receiver, he believed them to be from Mars as this was a popular theme at the time. In 1901, Tesla experimented with a crystal

---

[3] https://www.history.com/news/9-things-you-may-not-know-about-nikola-tesla

radio powered by electromagnetic waves[4]. He was so terrified by the resulting voices that came through that, though he was a scientist, he considered the possibility that it was the voices of ghosts. He wrote in his diary, "My first observations positively terrified me, as there was present in them something mysterious, not to say supernatural, and I was alone in my laboratory at night."

My parallel with Tesla, if I dare to compare myself with him at all, is that the beginning of his experiences followed a traumatic incident. I find this a common theme when speaking with others who have had

---

[4] https://www.mentalfloss.com/article/602456/thomas-edison-nikola-tesla-spirit-phone

similar encounters. Of course, his use of radios to attempt to communicate with unseen beings is often lauded as the beginning of paranormal investigation and those of us using our own version of these devices appreciate the commonality. It is always nice to compare yourself with a great mind, though I do realize he thought he was conversing with aliens for the most part.

The comparisons end there. Even though I am a member of MENSA, I am a much lower-level genius. Tesla was brilliant.

What is a Ghost Box?

A ghost box is not a telephone to the dead. It is, however, the next best thing.

At least we in the paranormal community tend to think so. Not everyone who looks to converse with the dead agrees, however. But it is a very popular tool.

A ghost box can come in several forms. The most common are made from older models, digitally tuned radios that have been altered or "hacked". While these radios still operate as they always did, the hack causes the radio to scan through channels without stopping and without blocking out the white noise either between channels or on those frequencies with no broadcast.

This is generally accomplished by either bending a pin, cutting a wire, or scratching away a trace on a mother board. This cancels the mute function which operates to help squash the white noise and stop the scan on the next strongest station coming through. Of course, a hacked radio will sometimes stop on a station however, depending on the model of radio and whether you have the antenna up or not (if it has an external antenna at all), it is rare.

Then there are the radios made from scratch by highly talented individuals with knowledge of electrical circuit boards and who can wield a soldering gun with a steady hand.

These old guard builders are revered in the community. While their ghost boxes were built to achieve the same output as a hacked radio, the methods they used were more akin to Mr. Tesla's crystal radios.

I do not possess such talents but have merely learned how to hack about six types of radios through trial and error and the watching (many times over) of instructional videos.

Some of the most popular radios that are used are the Radio Shack 12-587, 12-470, 20-125, and 12-150. Only certain, older models of each are hackable. The more talented among us utilize many more models. They solder wires and switches and achieve that glorious, noisy sweep of the channels that we all love so much.

I would be remiss if I did not mention the person considered the modern inventor of the ghost box. Mr. Frank Sumption built his "Frank's Boxes" and those who own them consider themselves very fortunate. Sadly, he passed away in 2014, however a book about his life and his work titled "Thinking Outside the Box: Frank Sumption, Creator of the Ghost Box" is available on Amazon.

My most recent ghost box acquisition is a beautiful, foam green dial radio hacked by someone who knew Frank and who owns several of his boxes. Both Steve and Katie Hultay display the same electrical engineering talent and, in my mind, are Frank's heirs apparent in the ghost box field. Of all the radios

I own, this one may turn out to be my favorite, not only for it's smooth sweep of the radio frequencies but for its pedigree as well.

Taking My Show On the…Tube

When I discovered what folks were sharing online, it was a game changer for me.

I had never known a way to share my own experiences, nor even considered doing so on such a public scale. Besides, there had never been any way to show tangible proof of what I had been encountering since I was five years old.

This was something I always just accepted. Until December of 2016, all of my stories were just that: stories. Not conversation starters, but for the right listener, a fascinating verbal slide down a rabbit hole that I'm sure entertained a few people over the years.

I was immediately taken by the possibility the ghost box radios offered as well as the thrill of sharing with others. My first box was a PSB7 ghost box. It is built for the purpose and so it is not a hacked radio, but one built with no mute circuit to begin with. It does not mute the white noise in between the frequencies, and it is built specifically for the spirits as a tool to communicate with us. It was made popular on that very well-known television show, and I was so excited when it arrived.

Even though I don't use it as much these days, I will always keep it as it was my very first radio.

PSB-7

Ghost Box Device

I began my YouTube channel using that box, and over time I managed to purchase a few other radios. My drawer is full of ruined boxes from a time when I thought soldering was something I might be able to accomplish. I can tell you that it is very easy, when soldering, to unsolder everything right next to what you are trying to solder. Do not underestimate soldering. It's hard. I'm bad at it. I do not solder anymore.

When I first discovered ghost box sessions and ITC, or instrumental trans-communication, I had already experienced a lifetime of dealing with my own form of spirit communication. I was only an unwilling spectator for a good part of my life. But life itself kept me busy.

I got married, had my children, worked, bought a business with my husband, and was a volunteer EMT for fifteen years. I did not think about anything paranormal on a regular basis. If something occurred, it occurred, and I moved on.

I cannot say why I was drawn to watch paranormal videos online. For some reason, something drew me to YouTube at one point, about seven years ago. I wasn't a huge consumer of these videos, so I don't recall why, but I happened upon some uploaded by a couple of individuals that were using very noisy radios that scanned without stopping. They claimed to be communicating with those in the spirit world. Their sessions and their "findings" were then shared with their viewers.

It was amazing to me because, up until then, I didn't believe there was any way to show tangible proof of what I had experienced for most of my life.

After binging on paranormal videos, I decided to give it a try. I had never actually initiated spirit contact, never asked for a specific spirit to come through. My hands had not even touched a Ouija board since I was thirteen years old. If contact was made, it came to me, unbidden, and I dealt with or simply ignored it.

What I witnessed others doing in these videos was such an overt, purposeful act: asking spirits to answer direct questions? Could it work?

My first videos and first sessions were simple. I didn't know what I was doing. I was mimicking those I'd watched. Basically, I did the sessions, did some basic editing with a free software program I found. In those days, it was possible to put annotations onto the videos directly on YouTube. I would add in what I thought I'd heard and upload them.

It's funny, looking back at those videos. I have done a flashback series on my channel and am amazed at how much I missed. What did the spirits think of me, blathering on and not responding to them? Hopefully, they forgave me for being such a noob.

I've bought many radios since and learned to hack a few radios myself. I'd like to think I've gotten better at these sessions, and I've had some very interesting messages come through over the years. Let me share some of the sessions and experiences that stand out from my glorious YT career.

Long Lost Love

When I go to parties, I try not to bring up the paranormal.

When the topic does come up, it usually does because my husband loves to instigate the conversation. We'll be at a gathering and he's looking for conversation starters. People are talking about their hobbies, and I can almost always tell when it's coming. He gets this look in his eyes, like the kid whose got the candy and can't wait to show it off.

I try, without offending him, to get him to stop but inevitably he will say "You want to know what my wife does?" And we're off to the races.

There are usually a couple of people who say they don't believe, and a glimmer of hope flares in me that the topic will be dropped. But it's usually overridden by those who are more than excited to start asking questions. Even the skeptics join in, most of the time. Inevitably, the questions turn toward contacting family.

"Oh, I had this one who passed away and I swear he came to me."

"Can you contact someone for me?"

Until recently, I had never done a session attempting to contact a specific spirit. However, during my sessions I have had the spirits of family members come through.

One of these sessions, and one of the

most surprising contacts I've had, occurred on St. Patrick's Day in 2017.

My house is a mother-daughter and my 88-year-old mom and her rescue cat, Abby, live with us. Her apartment is downstairs. Abby hates bags and most people. But she's a sweety.

On this particular night my mother was away and I thought it would be fun to do a ghost box session in moms apartment. I brought my Radio Shack 12-587, a very popular radio among paranormal "ghost hunters". It's a very simple radio and about thirty years old.

I had the radio in my left hand as I sat on mom's couch and my phone set up in front of me as a camera. Miss Abby sat watching from the loveseat. I started to film and welcomed everyone to the video with a basic explanation of what I'm about to do.

It was supposed to be the simplest of videos. This was early on in my YT career.

At one point, I asked if any spirit is around who watches over mom.

Suddenly, I hear a voice, a deep male voice, say "Yeah".

Now, if you watch this video, you will see the shocked look on my face because I recognized the voice.

The theory is that spirits can use the energy and voices in the radio transmissions to communicate with us.

But this voice did not come over the radio.

So, I said "Bill? Is that you?

And again, "Yeah".

If you watch the video, you may understand how it affected me. It has been 33 years since Bill passed and we still all miss him terribly. I was almost brought to tears. I did not tell my mother for three years because I didn't want to bring back any of the sadness from his passing. It hit me hard, but I'm very happy to know he's watching over her.

People do ask me about contacting family, and whether I think it's possible. When they remind me that "Houdini died and swore he'd come back, but never did", I don't have any answers for them.

Mom says a week after Bill passed, he

was standing in their master bedroom. It was the last time she saw him, and she felt he came to let her know he was okay. Thirty-three years later, he shows up in my session. I don't know how long he's been there, but I now just take for granted that he is watching over her. Perhaps love never truly dies.

A Question from Beyond

I've gotten a lot of interesting messages over the years. It takes time to be able to discern what is spirit contact and what is pareidolia which is, very basically, our human innate ability to make something out of something.

The actual definition of pareidolia is "the tendency to perceive a specific, often meaningful image in a random or ambiguous visual pattern".

Auditory pareidolia, then, is the same thing but with sound. We hear a sound, and our brains will flip through our cerebral reference library to make sense of what we're hearing.

It's the reason eyewitness accounts are often completely wrong. You can have an event and ten witness statements with each of them different from the last.

It's like having a loved one who always finishes your sentences. They hear one piece and their brain fills in the rest. Or it's like that old game of "telephone". Stand a group of people in a line and have the first person whisper a message into the second person's ear. Then down the line each person shares what they heard to the next person. By the end, the message often does not resemble the original at all.

Accusations of Pareidolia are nothing new to those in the paranormal community. We work to tune our ears and use our radios that are altered to continually scan through stations without stopping. The ability to discern "radio bleed" from actual spirit messages is vital.

Different people may hear different things when they listen. Be that as it may, it takes some time, and I trained my ear well but often the proof is in the video evidence itself.

I did a session one night with an old karaoke machine. Basically, it served as a colorful, glorified speaker. None of the fancy, lit-up boxes you see imbue the listener with any additional abilities, so don't be fooled by those who may try to convince you otherwise.

This particular night, I received a very interesting message. I watched it back many times. The radio did not stop on one channel. Every word in the message was said in a different voice as the radio scanned through the frequencies. I watched over and over trying to debunk it, but I could not. It said:

"Can I use this to talk to people."

When you're doing a ghost box session, sometimes you are concentrating so hard you miss things.

The original builder of the first ghost box, Frank Sumption, believed we should just let the box run. Don't ask questions. Let the spirits get used to it and try to send you messages.[5] We do it differently these days. We ask questions and hope we get answers.

This statement that came through was not a response to a direct question and I did not hear it in real time. But when I listened back, I was amazed. I remember editing this session and I just sat there in awe, playing it repeatedly.

---

[5] Sumption, Clune, Pfister, Davis, Thinking Outside the Box: Frank Sumption, Creator of the Ghost Box, January 17, 2019, Palmetto Publishing Group

I wished that I had heard it in real time so I could have answered whoever was asking. Whoever they are, I hope, in the following years, that they figured out that, yes, you can use this thing to talk to people.

Standing Guard for Eternity

Gettysburg is an amazing place.

Three days in July 1863 saw some of the worst fighting in the American civil war. It was a very important battle. If north had lost Washington would have fallen

I became friends with another YouTuber and we planned a trip to Gettysburg,

Pennsylvania to investigate the battlefields and other locations. Thus began our annual trips to this amazingly preserved historical place.

That first year, my husband couldn't come until the second day, so I drove down myself. The trip turned out to be a bit of a nightmare, but I will tell you about that in a later chapter.

I was exhausted when I finally arrived in Gettysburg but thrilled to meet my new friend. After we walked around and acclimated ourselves to the area, and had some dinner, I went to my room.

We stayed, and have stayed ever since, at the Gettysburg Inn B&B at The Dobbin House. It is a beautiful, rustic inn with a breakfast my friend swears by. In the restaurant, the staff wear period clothing, and the faire is also a throwback, albeit modernized, to the nineteenth century.

I was staying in the Lee room, which features a four-poster bed, and its own sitting room. After unpacking, I went to bed. It was probably only 9:30pm but it didn't take me long to fall fast asleep.

Sometime in the middle of the night, I woke up. As my eyes tried to adjust to the dim in the room lit only slightly from a light somewhere outside coming through the slats of the wooden blinds, I sensed that someone was standing next to the bed.

I know it may sound strange to you, but

my first instinct was to roll toward where I felt the presence. It did not occur to me that it could be a human being. This reaction is probably a result of a lifetime of finding someone or something inhuman standing next to my bed.

To my left, in front of the dresser, stands a soldier. He stood at attention, not looking at me but staring into the darkness beyond my bed. His uniform was nothing fancy, but it was obvious he was a military man.

I cannot emphasize my level of weariness that I was feeling. All I could think to say to this young man was "Sir I don't mind you being here. You may stand there all night, but I need to get some sleep. So, if you can allow me to do that, I would appreciate it."

As much as I would have liked to communicate with him, I could do nothing else but turn back to my right side and go to sleep. I was done. I was cooked.

I told my friend about the experience the next day and he lamented the missed opportunity as well.

Honestly, I don't think that soldier was there. I think he was a memory, and I don't think he was mine.

We will visit Gettysburg again this year, and I can't wait to go back.

Abandoned Farmhouse

One of my favorite investigations was of an abandoned home that belonged to the grandparents of a friend. It is just down the road from their second home in Pennsylvania. It has been sitting empty for 25 years because a decision could not be made about what to do with it. I asked if I could visit and have a session in the house.

She graciously allowed.

I packed up all my gear and she and another friend of ours and my daughter headed over.

I was flabbergasted. Even though shelves are collapsing, and it was messy and being used as storage, the dishes were still stacked in the cabinets, cutlery in the drawers.

We set up in the dining room and all walked the house. As we did, I recorded my friend telling the history of her family and the house. We went back downstairs to the wooden dining room table which had every family member's name carved on it.

I explained to them what we were going to do and rolled the camera. My friend's name is Vickey, and the other is Linda. As I started the introduction, Linda rolled her eyes up without moving a muscle. I turned and asked Linda what was wrong, and she replied, "the light is moving."

Vickey and I looked up at the old hanging light above us. It, indeed, had started to move. Nobody was upstairs, and we had been downstairs for over twenty minutes. We continued with the ghost box session, and we got some hits and some interesting messages. At one point, we heard a female voice say "bitches" which made us all laugh. Vickey said it was probably an aunt who used to live in the house.

When I eventually listened back to the audio, it turns out we were actually called witches.

The most interesting thing that came out of this investigation was one EVP (electronic voice phenomenon) I caught on my iPhone's microphone.

At one point before we went upstairs, I turned on the phone and began recording as I was setting up my camera equipment. Vickey was in the kitchen, and I heard her say she should take some things home with her since they were just wasting away.

On the video when I listen back, I hear a voice, angry, say "put that back!"

I was not running a radio at the time. It was not Vickey's voice, nor was it any of our voices. It was a voice that came out of nowhere.

When I told Vickey afterward, she said she was surprised and that it was probably that aunt again. Evidently the woman never liked visitors in the house when she was alive and still felt the same way!

A Hand on My Shoulder

My mother loves birds.

Her apartment makes up the entire bottom floor of our home and every square inch is covered with a lifetime of photographs, chachkas, and cat toys. It's a warm, inviting great grandma space with windows all along the back wall where her cat, Abby, sits and watches the bird feeders daily.

We can look down through a bay window in our kitchen at her back patio and watch her feathered friends enjoy their seeded buffet. She does get the occasional turkey family trapsing through as well as a plethora of renegade black and grey squirrels that swing from the feeder poles like a furry version of Cirque de Soleil. I've even caught one bear, lying on their back, cradling one of the feeders as it tried to break into it with his teeth.

Just for the record, we also get our fair share of deer, fox, and coyote in our neighborhood. That may come as a surprise to some, considering we live north of New York City, but it is very common around here. The local mantra is, "don't swerve, hit the deer!"

Don't come for me. It's a matter of safety. You are more likely to hurt yourself or your passengers if you swerve off the road and go into a ditch or hit a power pole. Cars can be repaired. Bambi's mom is adorable, but not worth that happening.

One sunny Saturday afternoon, I was home alone and just puttering around the house. As I came into the kitchen, something caught my interest outside, so I went over to the bay window and leaned over to look down at the feeding frenzy. Mom must have just put fresh seed out and that usually brought flocks of Blue Jays and smaller birds to the party.

As I leaned forward, I got the feeling someone was standing on my right side. You know that feeling. We can usually sense when another person has walked up beside us. That was what I felt.

As soon as that feeling registered, I felt a hand on my shoulder and I knew that whomever it was, was also leaning over to see what was going on below and outside.

My first response was to freeze as I stood, leant over the window seat. A moment later the feeling left, as if the invisible hand was lifted away, and I stood back up straight. Of course, there was nothing to see as I turned to my right, and I did not expect there to be.

I calmly called out, asking who was there, again not expecting an audible reply but just to let whomever it was know that I had sensed them, and I was interested to know who they were.

I am no doctor, but I imagine one could argue that, perhaps, I had just triggered a nerve in my shoulder or that I imagined the entire thing. But I do know what it feels like when someone puts their hand on my shoulder.

So, that evening while I was still alone in the house, I set up my Nikon Coolpix p600 camera on the counter in the kitchen. I sat it facing the bay window, now looking out at the darkness, in hopes I might pick up something to give me a clue to the identity of my earlier visitor.

The camera, like most digital 35mm cameras, has a very sensitive microphone. It was the camera I used for the first five years of my YouTube career, with much success.

I turned the camera on and left that side of the house altogether, so that I would not contaminate any audio I might pick up. About an hour later, I came back and turned it off, planning to go over the footage and audio the next day.

It is quite a tedious task to review video and audio recordings, especially when you are trying to listen for even the slightest of messages that might come through. There are also those in the field who will listen to their evidence played forward, backward, and at half speed or slower. There have been instances when preparing an eight-minute video has taken me over a week of days to prepare.

I hadn't expected to hear or see anything when I watched the video back. It is also rare to catch visual paranormal occurrences, contrary to popular belief, or what the television shows would have you believe. Audio evidence, good audio evidence, while also not as prevalent, is much more probable a result.

So, as I sat watching and listening to the footage of my dimly lit kitchen and the bay window, I was not all that hopeful for any results. To my surprise, there was one single minute on the video that surprised the heck out of me.

The first thing I heard was someone breathing, as if they were right next to the camera. Then, the camera moved just the slightest bit. It was as if someone was checking out the camera. Mind you, the camera was sitting flat on a granite countertop, right in the middle, and no human was anywhere near it.

I wish whomever it was had said something or that I had been doing a ghost box session at the time. I can only wonder if this visitor was my fellow bird watcher. I will never know.

Why I Do This

I've told you about ghost boxes, ITC (Instrumental Trans communication), and my sessions in which I believe I have heard voices from realms other than our own. Now I would like to describe for you how I do those sessions.

Before 2017, I had never attempted to specifically contact spirits, no less by the use of old, hacked digital transistor radios. My contact was random and came without warning. Some experiences were positive, such as when my mother-in-law came to me out of concern for my still-living father-in-law. Other times were not as positive, such as the awful whispers in the dark I suffered through in my twenties.

For fifty years, it never occurred to me that there would be a way to quantify and share my experiences. I saw no possibility of proving what was occurring to anyone who might have the slightest skepticism about this "gift". As far as I was concerned, it would always remain in the realm of the esoteric, scientifically unprovable, and only meant to be shared with a select few other human beings.

My first sessions were very simple. They still are, to this day. The equipment is also simple: old radios altered to scan without stopping in order to give the spirits and entities the opportunity to lace together words and sounds. Even the white noise comes through. With these things, it is theorized, communication may be possible between us and them.

The process and the equipment is simple for another reason. I believe it needs to be, if we wish to be believed what we are doing is real communication. The more complex the apparatus, in my opinion, the more it diminishes the plausibility of the endeavor.

In other words, the more a person "fancy's up" the tools they use, the more likely it appears they are trying to pull the wool over everyone's eyes.

My "portal" is a guitar amp, noise pedal, a Radio Shack 12-587 and lights for effect. A fancy speaker.

Smoke and mirrors have long been the cover under which charlatans have plied their trade. In the 1800's, medicine show hawkers sold bottles of "miracle" medicines that were usually colored water or high-proof alcohol. In the 1700's, Franz Mesmer treated his patients with his "proto-seances". While burning incense, and with music from the since-banned lead glass Armonica playing, he convinced those in need of medical care that he had cured them by manipulating their "animal magnetism".

    We have our own modern-day brand of medicine show folks in the paranormal community. But a fancy guitar speaker festooned with Christmas lights has no more ability to reach the spirit world than a simple digital recorder. These "portals", usually used in conjunction with a "ghost app" are akin to the fancy seances of old. Sadly, the apps are easily manipulated to spew only what the "investigator" wants their viewers to hear, and in these videos jump cuts also abound.

    I built my own setup using a small, portable guitar amp, a noise killer guitar pedal, power source, a Radio Shack 12-587 that I hacked myself, and some small lights which helped when doing sessions in the dark woods. All this amounts to a fancy speaker that looks really cool.

Spirit communication does not require you to spend hundreds or even thousands on equipment. Those few folks that I shared my experiences with simply had to take me at my word. ITC offered this amazing way to quantify what I was seeing and hearing. It offered a way for me to prove I wasn't crazy after all.

My sessions have evolved over time, but not necessarily in the way I perform them or the equipment that I use to do so. What has changed is my ability to hear the difference between radio transmissions and possible, actual spirit communication.

In other words, I have trained my ear.

At first, all I heard was the radio chatter, as it zipped by like a George Carlin stand-up set.

Patience is not a virtue I am particularly known for but that is what I had to practice as I learned to discern direct answers to my questions from all the other noise coming over the airwaves. That, of course, is the entire goal of the sessions. To ask a question and receive a direct response to said question. Or to receive a message so meaningful that it might just represent an entity reaching out on their own. The latter are rare, but they do occur. I've spoken of one in particular in which a nine-word statement was made with each word picked from a different transmission as the radio scanned quickly through the dial. Nine different voices strung together one imploring question, which I am very sad to have missed at the time.

After these many years, I recently went back and relistened to my first and earliest sessions. I am amazed at what I missed, and it saddens me that I could not reply to those trying to converse with me at the time.

How I Perform a Ghost Box Session

The first thing I do is decide where and when I will do a session. I have done these sessions at home, outside my home, in cemeteries, and in historic locations. It doesn't matter where you are because spirits are everywhere.

I once had someone tell me that they shower in the dark because they don't want spirits to see them naked. I found this funny because, if they are there, you can't do anything about it. Besides, if they are that bored, why deny them a little fun?

The most important thing about choosing where and when is that it's best to have a quiet environment. If your spouse is in the next room with the television blaring, or the kids are running around the house, you won't be able to quiet your own mind or hear what might be coming through either on your ghost box radio, or even directly to you from spirit.

Once I have made that decision, and I am sat in the quiet of my chosen moment, I will settle myself and sit in silence for at least fifteen minutes. This gives me an opportunity to clear my head of the day-to-day clamor that rules most of our lives and open myself to the spirits.

You may also find this time a good source of solace. It's a rare occasion, at least for me, that I have quiet time to myself these days. It's probably why I so enjoy visiting old cemeteries. They are peaceful, restful places where I usually go alone as most people don't enjoy them as much as I do.

So, you've sat for a bit, listening to the quiet, and now you are ready to start your session.

I generally bring a few types of equipment with me. I will have one of my hacked radios, my cell phone for recording the session, and one or more digital recorders.

To begin a session, I will welcome any spirit that may be around me at the time. There is no telling who or what might be around you at any given time. Even though I often visit historic cemeteries and graveyards, there is not a reason to think that those who repose there would still be present.

A grave at Bonaventure Cemetery, Savannah Georgia – Digital Recorder Session by Ray

There are those in the paranormal field that believe there is a hierarchy to the afterlife and that we can only speak to those who exist in the lower realms. It is also said that, as time goes by, a spirit may ascend to a higher level and, thus, become harder, if not impossible, to reach. You can read more about this in a book titled "When Spirits Speak: Live Spirit Ghost Box Communication" by my friend Bruce Halliday.

Bruce has been involved in the paranormal for decades and speaks often to two specific spirit guides who have explained the system to him.

While I am welcoming the spirits, I will begin recording on my phone and turn on the ghost box. Recording is important as you will need to listen back afterwards. It will be difficult, especially at first, to catch any and all messages what might come through.

Don't be dismayed if you hear nothing. This might happen many times before you receive a direct answer to one of your questions. Both you and the spirits around you must acclimate to the new connection you are trying to form.

When I ask questions, I give the spirits time to answer. I have been to locations with other investigators, in which we have done a round-robin questioning of spirits. Too often, some of them will ask questions one after the other without leaving adequate time for a response.

Remember, you are recording. Do not become impatient. Even if you do not hear an answer, one may have been given that you will pick up later, either when you listen back to your radio recording or to your digital recorder.

Try to give yourself at least a half an hour for a session. Once the spirits sense you are open to them, you may have greater success. At the end of the session, thank those that have come through and show your appreciation. I do not believe it is an easy feat for them to do so.

If you wish to share your sessions, there are a number of free video editing software programs available online. I use one called VSDC and it works wonderfully. There is a bit of a learning curve, but there are also many videos online to teach you how to use it efficiently.

Now, let's talk about what you should not do.

Demons and the Paranormal Entertainer

There are what I call "paranormal entertainers" who purport to do the same thing we do, however, many of them covet views, likes, and subscribers more than they do actual experiences.

They will piece together their video "evidence" to make it appear as if they have achieved mind-blowing contact with the spirit world. These same folks see demons around every corner.

Real sessions should be recorded and presented without breaks or "jump cuts". A jump cut is an editing trick in which the presenter will show the question being asked and then cut to a recording of a presumed direct answer to the same question.

They have simply cut the video and added in a recording, possibly from another time or, in many cases, recorded specifically for the video. Sometimes, it may be their own voice answering them, just slowed so that it cannot be identified as such. Others with more technical ability will manipulate a ghost box app and add in their own recordings which, when played back, sound like direct responses from the spirit world.

Conversely, those who consider themselves true students of the paranormal, or perhaps paranormal investigators, who are testing the theory that we can communicate at all using the equipment we have, seem boring in comparison. Popular paranormal television shows and celebrities are partly to blame for this phenomenon. Sadly, many of these folks make a good deal of money from the platforms they are on, so there is probably not much chance of that changing anytime soon.

The only time I will cut a scene is if I have not heard anything for some time. But there should never be a cut right after a question is asked.

There are other methods the entertainers use to fake paranormal contact. One is called masking, in which video of something occurring by the hand of the presenter is laid over a video of the same location with the string pulling the chair or the hand throwing the ball masked out. It is also not very difficult to overlay a shadow figure over a video of someone sleeping in a supposedly haunted house.

Of course, paranormal chicanery has been around for more than one hundred years. From the early table knocking to faked photographs from the 1800s, it has proved itself a lucrative undertaking. You just need the guile and lack of conscience to do it.

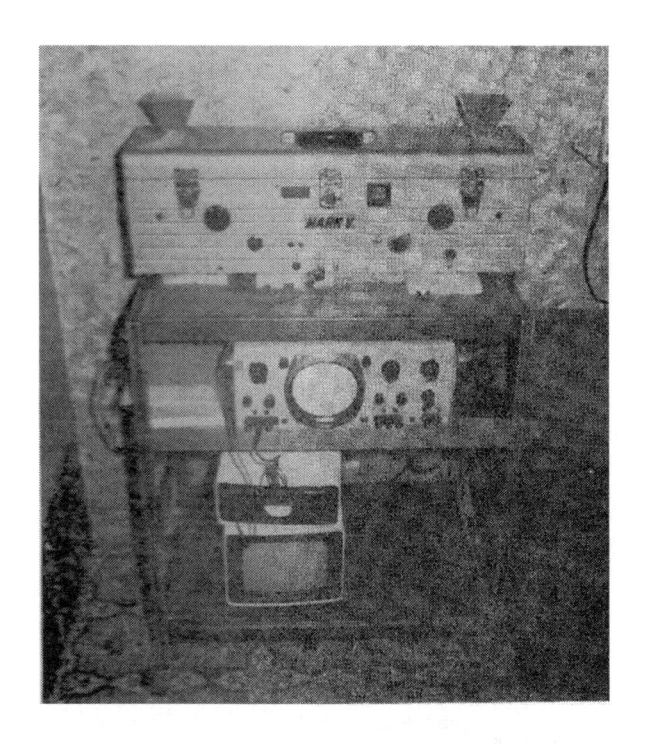

Spiricom Mark V, a hoax from the 1970's

It's Not What You Believe, it's what you Believe Might Be Possible

In the last four decades, there have been over 450 studies done researching the connection between paranormal beliefs and cognitive functioning. Only a sixth of them have met the inclusion criteria of The National Library of Medicine.

Even so, just the fact that they have been done at all is both surprising and feels like a step forward for those involved in the paranormal.

It is a double-edged sword, in my opinion. While those who have experienced paranormal happenings hope for scientific proof of what they have seen, heard, and felt, it is more than obvious that the scientific and medical communities do these studies for another reason. Their goal, it seems, is to provide a physiological or psychological explanation thus rendering it a malady to be treated and possibly corrected.

It is possible that there is no cure.

There is a term we hear often, and it refers to a tendency humans have to perceive "a specific, often meaningful image in a random visual pattern." The term is pareidolia (para-dol-ee-uh) and the form of this we are accused of often is "auditory pareidolia" wherein a person may perceive or interpret sounds or patterns in white noise that are not actually there.

Medical literature, historically, listed this as a malady known as apophenia or "musical ear syndrome" and, not surprisingly, discussed whether those having these experiences were suffering from a mental disorder.

There is also something called "face pareidolia" which is an illusion wherein we perceive a face when one is not there, such as in the clouds or seeing Jesus in a burnt piece of toast.

It seems that we humans are always trying, even on a subconscious level, to make sense of the things we are looking at or hearing. Someone called it the "human face-detection system." Our nature is to make order from chaos: to be able to understand what is in front of us so that we then know how to deal with it. It's an innate safety mechanism of the human psyche.

These phenomena have been extensively researched and studied for the same reason the occur at all. Scientists and medical personnel feel the need to understand what is happening so that they may label it, address it, and move on to the next problem.

During my YouTube career, I have received comments from skeptics. Some of them ask questions politely while others choose to denigrate what I and my peers do. I don't usually respond to the negative comments however, if I am doing a live stream and this occurs, I have a simple answer I give them.

A theory is an idea, an explanation, of something that is not yet a fact but is accepted until it is disproven. It is based on available data. The theory we work under is that we may be able to speak to spirits and other entities using mechanical means, such as a scanning radio, white noise, or just recording apparatus. The data we base it on are our own experiences.

Those of us who have had these experiences have formed our own hypothesis, that being our assumption that this can truly work. The difference between the theory and our hypotheses is that the latter is merely based on our beliefs, and they serve as the impetus for

us to keep trying.

Occam's Razor

In doing my research for this book, I found that many surveys asking if people believe in the paranormal have been done over the years. Their validity comes into question as they have been commissioned by some very interesting yet non-paranormal related companies and individuals.

The consensus, however, seems to be that approximately fifty percent of Americans believe in the paranormal and a third of the country believe in UFOs.

There are surveys from other countries that show even higher percentages that are gender specific, such as Japan. In 2013 a survey there resulted in 50% of the male participants believing in ghosts while 64% of the women believe the same.

I have my own opinion, of course. After a lifetime of experiences, I still question it all sometimes. But I come back to this: I am a (seemingly) stable human being, with a home, a family, a business, hobbies, and friends. There is nothing special about me nor have I ever given the impression that I am left of center in any way, yet these things have happened to me since I was five years old.

Is it possible to be normal in every single way, but one?

Occam's Razor (or Ockham's Razor) is a principle attributed to a 14th century friar named William of Ockham. A later translation of it reads "Entia non sunt multiplicanda praeter necessitate" and I try to live by it.

Basically, what it means to most people is that the simplest explanation for something is usually the correct one.

Keeping this in mind, let's go back to those surveys. In 2023, there are 334,233,854 people living in the United States. More than three quarters of those are adults, so let's round down to 258 million adults.

According to the survey, let's say fifty percent of those folks either believe in the paranormal or have had some sort of encounter.

That would mean over 120 million people are either really encountering something paranormal, or they are suffering from a very specific mental illness. This malady would only affect them in this one specific way yet not affect their lives in any other manner.

Perhaps it could be called the "Ghost Gene."

These are the thoughts I have when I start to question my own experiences. At least, based on those surveys, and if I do have the ghost gene, I am not alone.

My Paranormal Partner in Crime: Dr. Ray
(no crimes were committed in the making of this book)

When I first started to record my ghost box sessions, I had no idea I would make a friend, let alone one of my best friends.

In 2016, I was not all that aware of the online video sharing platforms. Yes, I had a Myspace page about twenty years ago. And yes, I do have a Facebook page, but I probably have the lowest friend count of anyone out there. I considered it a place to share with family and my closest friends. I did not then, and do not now, friend every person that hits me up with a request.

Looking at the life happenings of strangers just seems like voyeurism to me, like I'm peeping into the lives of people I hardly know, and for which I have no business doing.

Discovering YouTube was akin to someone in their seventies finally understanding what a meme is. I realize now how thoroughly the paradigm has shifted. While typing this page, the grammar checker flagged Myspace, but not YouTube or meme.

I may have touched on this earlier. If so, I am sorry. Blame it on old age.

My videos began somewhat inauspiciously with me sitting on the couch, or the floor, running my PSB-7 and recording as I asked questions and waited for answers. I had zero knowledge of video or audio editing, nor did I have much fashion sense or any awareness of how I looked or sounded on camera. Take my word for it: I'm no wiz now nor am I a fashion plate, but I like to think I've improved somewhat.

    I published my first videos in December of 2016, and began watching those of others doing the same. Four months later, in April of 2017, and unbeknownst to me, another YouTube paranormal channel featured part of one of my videos. His name is Dr. Ray Clark, and he had a weekly show where he shared uploads from other paranormal channels such as mine.

I don't remember how I became aware of his live streams. At this point, I was spending time in the chat rooms of other paranormal content creators and my screen name began to be recognized among those with which I interacted, many of whom followed my channel as a result. One of them must have alerted me to his "This Week in ITC" broadcasts and I joined the chat one evening.

Little did I know that this was the beginning of a close friendship, not only between him and I but our spouses as well.

Dr. Ray Clark and the author, investigating an abandoned Oddfellow theater in Bay City, Michigan

Ray is also the reason I decided to give live streaming a try myself. In November 2017, I went live with a ghost box session using my Radio Shack, one of my favorite radios. It didn't get many views, but it was fun, and I had Ray to thank for even giving it a try.

Going forward, Ray shared my videos often on his live streams. We became fast friends, and, in July of 2018, planned a trip to Gettysburg, Pennsylvania to investigate the battlefields and haunted locations in that storied town.

I have always been that person who tells everyone I know, and anyone who will listen, that you need to be very wary of the people you meet online. You need to travel the internet in stealth mode and certainly not meet up with someone you only know from your monitor or phone.

Mind you, I was also the chick in 1986 with one of the first personal computers going into those archaic chat rooms. I also frequented those old 800 numbers you could call and be part of a party chat. You would dial in and suddenly be in a "room" with multiple voices and conversations you would have to jump right into. I ended up going on two blind dates because of these shenanigans. One of the dates went well. We went to a French restaurant, on the east side, the food so tiny we went to McDonalds afterwards. He was a very nice guy, but not really my type. I never saw him again. That feels like a lifetime ago.

      The plan for the 2018 trip was to meet up with Ray and it included my husband, with Ray's wife not making the trip. But something at work came up and I had to drive to Gettysburg myself with my spouse coming down the next day. I set out in my car, got an hour down the road, just over the GW bridge, when a warning light came on in the car, alerting me to low oil pressure and that I needed to shut down the car immediately. This had happened a couple of weeks before, but we thought it had been remedied.

    I can't think of a worse spot to have this happen. When you exit the George Washington Bridge on the New Jersey side, the traffic situation is less than optimal. Your fellow New Yorkers give you no quarter. Anyone who has ever driven it will attest to this. I was quite distraught and called my husband. The last thing I wanted to do was seize the engine on my Audi A4.

The only option I had was to turn back home and hope the car made it that far. It did but I lost at least two hours on the trip. I got home, jumped into our other car, and took off again.

The trip from our home to Gettysburg usually takes about four hours. I was using my GPS but, at some point, traffic backed up somewhere in the hinterlands of Pa. I tried to adjust my directions, even pulling off somewhere a couple of times to reassess this journey and my entire decision to make the trip at all. Was this a sign from the universe? I did finally arrive but what was supposed to be a four-hour trip ended up being a nine-and-a-half-hour disaster of an adventure.

You must understand something about my friend, Dr. Ray. He is an economical speaker and he has an uncanny ability to look on the bright side of any situation. You would think him a student of the great stoics. If he can't control it, he does not let it phase him.

Exiting my car on that afternoon in Gettysburg, after screaming into my windshield for all those hours, I may have looked like a bedraggled mess, but Ray's calm demeanor helped me to downshift back into my normal, human form and we had an amazing time after that.

We had a that evening and most of the next day before my husband was able to join us, so we were able to visit Sach's covered bridge, a location considered haunted by many, through which the confederate army retreated after the Battle of Gettysburg in 1863.

    The following day, we decided to go looking for a garage sale. We had seen signs for the sale and we were always on the hunt for old radios to use in our sessions. We never found the sale, but we inadvertently came upon the old Black's Graveyard. This turned out to be quite lucky and you can see the video on my YouTube channel. We had quite a good session there.

My husband did join us shortly after that session and we enjoyed the rest of the time in Gettysburg. We visited Little Round Top, which looks down over The Devil's Den. Bloody fighting took place there with snipers above and below, and a final rush up the hill by the southern forces who were decimated by the Union troops rushing back down at them with bayonets affixed after they ran out of ammunition.

We live streamed from the Devil's Den and the National Cemetery, both on my cell phone. The cell service was iffy, but we had an amazing time.

Dr. Ray at Little Round Top, Gettysburg Battlefield, Gettysburg, Pennsylvania

It has been six years now, and we have made the trek to Gettysburg every year together since. Ray and his wife and myself and my husband are now close friends, paranormal investigating notwithstanding. We visited them in Michigan, and they visit us in New York. Our spouses are now lovingly known as Spouse Paranormal, as they each have their own opinions of what we do. They show a considerable amount of patience while maintaining a healthy sense of humor and Ray and I appreciate them more than they know.

Haunted Sach's Bridge, Gettysburg
August 2018 and October 2020

Sach's Covered Bridge, Gettysburg, Pennsylvania

We have visited the Sach's bridge every year we have been to Gettysburg. Sometimes Ray would get up at 5:30 in the morning to be there in the quiet of the day, before other visitors would converge on this popular location.

The Sachs Covered Bridge has also been known as Sauck's Covered Bridge and the Waterworks Covered Bridge. It's a 100-foot truss covered bridge that sits over Marsh Creek between Cumberland and Freedom Townships in Adams County, Pennsylvania.

While the bridge was going through a half-a-million-dollar restoration in 1996, a flash flood knocked it from one of its supports. It cost an additional $100,000 and took another year to repair the damage.

During the battle of Gettysburg, which took place July 1-3, 1863, this bridge was crossed by regiments of both the Union (on the way in) and Confederate (on the way out) armies. It was designated as Pennsylvania's most historic bridge in 1938 and closed to vehicular traffic in 1968.

The paranormal connection to this location comes in the form of one story, told two ways, each placing blame on opposing sides in the American Civil war.

The story goes that either during the Battle of Gettysburg, or during the retreat, three men were either found to be deserters by confederate army officers or they were southern soldiers dressed in union uniforms discovered by the northern forces. Both stories end with the three of them being hung from the bridge as traitors but there is no clear answer to confirm which version is true or if the stories are true at all.

The author at Sach's Bridge, Gettysburg

Modern ghost hunters and even some folks not involved in the paranormal have had experiences on the bridge. There have been photographs that supposedly show floating heads or full bodied apparitions of soldiers. Others have smelled cigar smoke or heard distant musket fire.

One experience, which Dr. Ray duplicated for himself, is that of a spirit smoking a cigarette. The object was to set a lit cigarette on one side of the bridge and watch as an unseen smoker puffed on the offering.

On one of his early morning visits to the bridge, this worked for Dr. Ray, though he did not get it on video. I believe him unequivocally as Dr. Ray is not one to lie, on any occasion.

We have done several sessions on the bridge, with some interesting results. There is also a field just below the bridge called the meadow. One of the late-night ghost hunts Ray and I went on brought us there.

It was on this occasion that two things happened. I was walking about fifteen feet behind Ray on a path that runs along this very woodsy area. It was late at night and most of the others in the group had already entered the wooded area. I felt a voice in my right ear. It was a male voice and he said, in a very seductive manner, "Hello there."

I stopped immediately and looked around, really figuring one of the others had come up next to me, though I couldn't imagine why any one of them would do that as they were all strangers to me.

Ray realized I was no longer following him, and he doubled back. I told him what had happened and, in his usual relaxed manner, thought it was "very cool."

At that point, and at that spot, we decided to turn on one of our ghost box radios and see if we could get any sort of explanation for what had happened. No explanation was forthcoming however a voice came through and said it was "Steve", seeming to confirm this with a number of additional messages such as "it's me" and "it's him."

Ray realized it was his very good friend who had passed away.

I do not think the voice in my ear was Ray's friend, but I do think Ray was glad to hear his friend's voice. It is a rare occurrence to hear from someone you knew or even a specific someone you might be asking for or about. When it does happen, it can be overwhelming, moving, and surprising.

Ray once again thought it was very cool.

Late Night Xtreme Ghost Hunt
July 2019
The 100 Degree Attic

We seem to love going to Gettysburg in the summer, and 2019 was no different. It works for outdoor investigations, except for the bugs, of course. What you need to take into consideration is this: if it's ninety degrees Fahrenheit outside, what might the temperature be inside?

This year, we signed up for the Late-Night Xtreme Ghost Hunt with a local company called Gettysburg Ghost Hunts. They have access to some locations we would not be able to get into on our own so it made sense. The hunt begins at 11:30pm and runs into the early morning hours.

One of the locations we went to was a building, an old home, that was used as a field hospital during the battle. Of course, many of the homes in Gettysburg were commandeered as field hospitals or officer's quarters in 1863. This was just one of them. There was no power to the house, so our lights were all we had to see our way around.

Ray, I, and our spouses headed in and were looking around upstairs when someone mentioned there was an attic. My husband's first reaction was "nope, we're not going in the attic." The man has the presence of mind to consider the temperature inside vs outside question. I looked at Ray and, of course, he was already looking for the staircase.

My husband did acquiesce, of course, because he is a supportive partner, and we headed up to the attic.

When we pushed the door to the attic open, a wave of heat hit us. It was stifling, dusty, and smelled of old and forgotten places. It was hard to breathe. On the floor sat two baby dolls, which really seemed out of place.

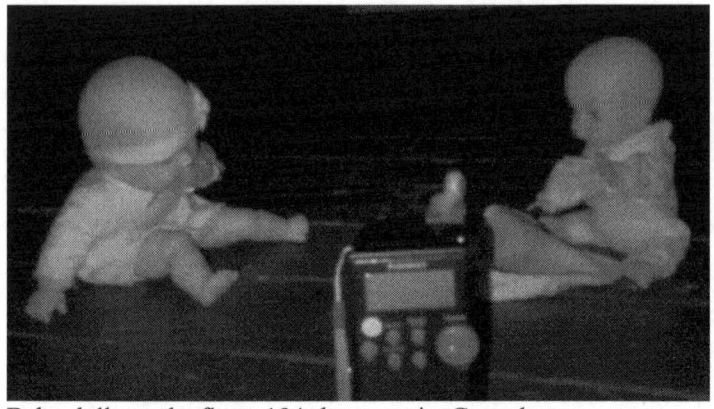

Baby dolls on the floor, 104-degree attic, Gettysburg

Ray and I walked to the right side and sat down. I set up my phone to begin filming and Ray set down the ghost box radio. Across from us, I could hear my husband in the dark saying it was actually one hundred four degrees in the attic. Ray's wife lay flat on the floor, trying to stay as low as possible to save herself. She's a champ.

After our time in the oven of an attic, we all sat in a circle on the dusty first floor with our guide, around a PSB-7 ghost box and proceeded to ask questions. I was filming with my infrared camera and caught an orb as it dove down directly into the radio. You can see this video on my YouTube channel as well. We had a good session and were glad to be able to breathe normally again.

Bonaventure Cemetery
Savannah, Georgia
July 2021

I have visited many cemeteries during the last seven years. I am what is known as a taphophile. So is Dr. Ray, for that matter. It means "a person interested in cemeteries." They run the gamut, from well-kept, ornately landscaped to forgotten by time and almost unrecognizable.

Our crew visited Bonaventure Cemetery in Savannah, Georgia in the July of 2021. I had been there once before and wanted Dr. Ray to experience the place. It is amazing.

We were told by a local that the art students at the local college, SCAD, like to have picnic lunches there. It is understandable, at least to the likes of us. The place is amazing.

The best way I can describe its layout is what appears to me like small neighborhoods. There are graves for people from all over the world and huge family plots. The massive live oak trees are covered in Spanish moss which, on an overcast day, makes the place look like a Victorian daguerreotype.

Ray in Bonaventure Cemetery, Savannah, Georgia

At Bonaventure, there is the well-known grave of a little girl named Gracie Watson. Hers is maybe the most popular in the cemetery. Her story is a sad one.

In the 1880s, her parents, W.J. and Frances Watson ran the Pulaski House Hotel off Johnson Square in Savannah, Georgia. Gracie had the run of the hotel and was very popular with the guests. Unfortunately, she passed away right before Easter when she was six years old from pneumonia.

Devastated by her loss, her father commissioned a sculptor named John Walz to carve her monument, which he did using a photograph as a reference.

There have been stories of the statue crying bloody tears and of some claiming to see Gracie's ghost in Johnson Square where her parent's hotel used to stand.

The postscript to her story is probably the saddest part. After her death, her father quit his job at the Pulaski hotel. He worked at another hotel for a short time but then he and his wife moved back to New England. They left Gracie behind in both life and in death as they are both buried up north as well.

Ray and I, and our willing spouses, have visited many other interesting, possibly haunted locations. Among them are:

Letchworth Village – the now closed psychiatric hospital in Rockland County, New York

Jenny Wade House – the house where the only civilian killed during the Gettysburg battle fell.

Eisenhower or Suicide Bridge – Gettysburg, considered haunted but nobody ever died there

Antietam and Harpers Ferry – American Civil War battle locations

The Grove – A battle location in Gettysburg no longer open to paranormal investigators.

Sleepy Hollow Cemetery – the resting place of Washington Irving and his headless horseman

Battlefields of Gettysburg – The Triangular Field, Cemetery Ridge, The Peach Orchard, Wheatfield, McPherson Ridge, Seminary Ridge, and more

    We are looking forward to more travels in the future. If you get the chance to visit any of these places, you will enjoy them even more if you do some research before you go. The stories are amazing.

In Conclusion

Six months ago, we lost our Yorkshire terrier of seventeen years. Gizmo was a good boy, and he was very popular with the spirits whenever I would do a ghost box session. They would often call out to him through my hacked radios, and I wondered if he would come to visit once he crossed the rainbow bridge.

Recently, my sixteen-month-old grandson and his mom were visiting. They have their own pets at home: one skittish cat and one very excitable boxer. Whenever Little Brendan sees a dog anywhere, he lights up, points, and makes what seems like very positive sounds that we imagine are like words to him as he is not verbal yet. The little man loved Gizmo as well.

This day, he was toddling around the living room. I was talking to my daughter-in-law who was standing in the kitchen nearby.

As we were speaking, he let out that same happy sound and pointed to a spot on the floor in front of him. His mother remarked that it was the way he usually pointed at a dog when he would see one. Just as she said this, he leaned down and began to pet, from front to back, an animal that was not there. We both watched in shocked silence for a few seconds.

I asked him if Gizmo was there. He just smiled at me and went back to playing.

The moment was bittersweet. It seemed that Gizzy might have come around to say hello to his boy one more time.

I know it is said children often have a second sight, a brief gift that fades away as they grow older. I have been told that all my life. It did not work out that way for me, but I have often thought about what it might mean, if it is truly something that occurs.

Could it be the last, soft tether to the other side from which we came and, once we are firmly, securely, stuck on this side of the veil, does it get retracted until it is time for us to return? Is it always there, and most of us just can't see it?

Am I just crazy?

I still ask myself that question.

But…nah.

There have been times when I have envied those who do not have these experiences. I have always called them "blissfully ignorant" but in the nicest way possible. I see it as akin to how I feel about aliens. If you don't want to believe that there are scary, awful, frightening, demonic entities that can do horrible things to you that you can't control, I don't blame you at all. Why would you want that in your life? If you don't want to believe in it, why would you want some person who says they see dead people trying to convince you that you should?

It took me many years to get past the fear and confusion surrounding my experiences and I would not wish it on anyone, even if it would help prove what I have gone through.

The goals I set for myself when I decided to write this book were very simple.

First, I wanted to leave behind my story for those who matter to me most in this world. I have made peace with the possibility that my family members may be the only folks that will buy copies, at my urging, of this book. If that happens, I'm good with it. Okay, maybe not, but I'll live. If you are reading this and we are not related, I really appreciate you!

Second, I have wanted to share my experiences, both from my life in general and from my online YouTube channel, for some time. I realize that these experiences, which I have always perceived to be paranormal, may be looked upon by others as abnormal. Still others may believe my stories to be just…stories. I assure you they are as real to me as anything you may have been through in your life, but you only have my word on that, and I don't expect anything more from you than your enjoyment of this book.

And finally, one of my greatest life's goals has been to be a published author. Just seeing this book in print will fulfill this lifelong dream. I am working on a novel. It is a longer work of fiction, a ghost story that I've been working on for some time. Thanks to a long bout of crushing self-doubt, it's been on the back burner for some time. I am hoping that getting this book published will reawaken my drive so that I can bring you that story, which I truly believe is so much more entertaining than my life story.

One More Thought

Charlatans in the paranormal field have been around for hundreds of years. Traveling medicine show barkers and snake oil salesmen peddling their wares, crystal ball and table readers and more have been around for centuries. There will always be someone who will try to convince you that something magical is real.

I believe it is because they play upon the hope that all humans harbor within them.

No matter what you believe or do not believe, no matter who you believe in or do not believe in, you have hope. You have hope for yourself, for your loved ones, your friends, your pets, the world, yourself. You may even have hope for what comes after this life, or you may just be hoping for a better tomorrow.

Here is what I hope for you, which is what I hope for myself: Calm smooth days where you are enough, and the ability to fulfill every request made of you and still have quiet time left for yourself to sit quietly and just be.

Thank you for reading my book. It means the world to me.

THE END

Made in the USA
Middletown, DE
30 September 2024